New Religious Movements in the Catholic Church

D0869419

NEW RELIGIOUS MOVEMENTS IN THE CATHOLIC CHURCH

edited by
Michael A. Hayes

BURNS & OATES
A Continuum imprint
LONDON • NEW YORK

Burns & Oates
A Continuum Imprint
The Tower Building
11 York Road
London SE1 7NX

15 East 26th Street
New York
NY 10010

www.continuumbooks.com

First published 2005

British Library Cataloguing-in-Publication Data
A catalogue record for this book is available from the British Library.

ISBN 0–86012–384–7

Typeset by RefineCatch Limited, Bungay, Suffolk
Printed and bound by MPG Books Ltd, Bodmin, Cornwall

Contents

Acknowledgements

I am very grateful once again to Robin Baird-Smith and his colleagues at Continuum for publishing these essays. I also wish to thank St Mary's College through its Research and Scholarship Fund, and *The Tablet* Trust, for generous grants that were made available for this project to bear fruit. A special word of thanks to Dr Arthur Naylor, and to my colleagues in the School of Theology, Philosophy, and History especially Maria Dowling and Carol Lourdas, and Anthony Towey.

Michael A. Hayes
First Sunday in Advent 2004

Abbreviations

AIDS	Acquired Immune Deficiency Syndrome
CCC	Catechism of the Catholic Church
CCR	Catholic Charismatic Renewal
CSCO	Centre for Study of Christian Origins
DH	Denzinger
DNA	Deoxyribonucleic acid
EE	*Ecclesia in Europa*
FC	*Familiaris Consortio*
GS	*Gaudium et spes*
HAART	Highly Active Anti-Retroviral Therapy
HIV	Human Immunodeficiency Virus
ICCRS	International Catholic Charismatic Renewal Services
TB	Tuberculosis
UNESCO	United Nations Educational, Scientific and Cultural Organisation

Foreword

Having been present at most of the lectures in this second series on Mission and Evangelization, I can bear witness to the diversity that they represent, albeit around a common theme in 'the vision of the ecclesial movements'.

This second series of lectures in 2003–04 complements the first series given a year earlier by cardinals on their vision, mission and evangelization. Across both series a particular attraction was that diversity of experience and cultural context for mission and evangelization which were presented and explored by the contributors. I am sure that Michael Hayes is right in his suggestion to the reader not to try to compare and contrast the lectures but to see them as different insights into mission and evangelization – a simple yet profoundly significant challenge to Christian living today.

I would again wish to thank Michael Hayes for his vision, energy and expertise in planning this second series of lectures. He did well to bring to St Mary's College, Strawberry Hill, the founders and those with close links to the foundation of ecclesial movements to deliver these lectures, and to carry the project forward so quickly into print.

Arthur Naylor

Introduction

Michael A. Hayes

One of the signs of a healthy congregation is the simple variety of people which it includes. All sorts of people from different backgrounds, with different outlooks and different insights and experiences. I think that is a real sign of hope and promise. In this collection of essays we have something of that great variety, many different backgrounds, outlooks and different insights and experiences. And yet all have as their main thrust a simple and perennial question: 'How best do I live the Gospel today?' The various ecclesial movements represented here offer a response to that question, and the variety of responses we have is, I suggest, diverse, like that of a healthy congregation.

These essays came out of a series of lectures at St Mary's College, Twickenham, offered during 2003–04 on the topic 'Mission and Evangelization'. They were an attempt to offer some vision in response to John Paul II's call for a 'New Evangelization'. This was the second series of lectures on this subject, the earlier series being given by some of the cardinals of the Church from around the world, offering their particular understanding of the need and task of evangelization in the Church today. The lectures contained in this volume offer a response to the same challenge in the Church, from the perspective of the ecclesial movements. The speakers came from movements that are represented across the world in many different countries. They included the founders of movements, active members and those who have been responsible for articulating the specific insights of the movements.

Some of these essays are simply the story of the movement thus far, and like all good stories they invite us to reflect and draw out key ideas. Some offer a reflection on the theological foundations of the movements; and some offer us a cultural and theological reflection on the Church and Christian life today through the particular perspective of the spirituality of that movement.

As Charles Whitehead reminds us, we are not dealing with a very precise term when we talk of 'ecclesial movements', and he offers us some common themes, but warns us not to try to fit all of them into similar structures. The divergences are as many as the convergences. That great range of types of structure is well represented here. The Community of Sant'Egidio is a loosely knit community, where gathering for prayer and working for the poor identify the members. The Community of the Beatitudes invites married couples to be part of its movement and formally to consecrate themselves. Some movements include lay, consecrated and ordained members; some include whole families; some live formally in community, while others do not. The community of L'Arche can include members of other faiths or no faith at all.

At the same time as this diversity there are common themes that bring these movements together. Either explicitly or implicitly they find a point of reference in the Second Vatican Council with its universal call to holiness and to the active apostolate. Kiko Argüello tells us this is an imperative: 'We are one of the new realities which are bringing the Council to the parishes, and to implement the Council is a matter of life and death for the Church.' The movements recognize a 'charismatic' dimension to the Church that complements the institutional dimension. Whitehead quotes John Paul II as saying: 'There is no conflict or opposition in the Church between the institutional dimension and the charismatic dimension.' The ecclesial movements all seek to articulate the spirituality and explore the nature of the lay member of the Church not simply in negative terms – one who is not ordained or religious. And all recognize that in seeking to live the Christian life, the faithful are called to be people who evangelize, because that is part of the Christian mandate and an essential – and urgent – one, our writers would insist. 'The contribution of the lay faithful to the life of the Church is essential: they have an irreplaceable role in the proclamation and the service of the Gospel of hope' (John Paul II, *EE* 41).

The foundations and roots of these movements similarly draw on common sources for nourishment and inspiration.

Many of these are, of course, the heritage of all Christian life, such as pondering the Word of God. Others can be seen as real signs of encouragement to the rest of the Church – the need to pray together, to build loving relationships, the call to serve the poor, the recognition of the importance of Christian witness by the way of living. Whitehead talks of those who, while being loyal committed members of the parish, are seeking some richer experience of faith. Some invite a new reflection such as the key role of Mary in Christian lay spirituality and the role of suffering in the life of members of the Church. Chiara Lubich describes a 'Marian profile' of the Church which offers the prophetic and charismatic dimension. Luis Fernando Figari describes Mary as the 'bearer and educator of Christian life'. Kiko Argüello insists that suffering is an inherent part of mission which is carried out 'not by preaching, but by being crucified. This is the tradition of the Church.'

In reading these various essays one constantly comes back to the essential link of *kerygma*, *koinonia* and *diakonia* in the life of the Church, each nourishing, and being nourished by, the others. The movements, with their community dimension, can easily be seen as specific examples of communion within the Church (*koinonia*); and often their specific work (e.g. L'Arche with people with disabilities, Sant'Egidio with the poor) is seen as the Church at the service of humanity (*diakonia*). Mario Marazziti and Austen Ivereigh quote Cardinal Martini describing a 'living synthesis of the primacy of God, of prayer, and of listening to the Word; of taking God's word seriously and, at the same time, of dedicating oneself in a concrete, effective way to the poor'. And from this synthesis comes a proclamation of the Good News (*kerygma*), for as John Paul II says in *Redemptoris Missio* (42), 'the witness of Christian life is the first and irreplaceable form of mission'. In their members the ecclesial movements enable Christians to live out this threefold life of communion, service and evangelization; and for the rest of the Church they offer an invitation to reflect and enter more deeply into the mystery of the life with Christ.

*

This collection offers a rich range of insights and resources for reflection on 'A New Evangelization' through the prism of the ecclesial movements. For some of these essays the starting-point is the situation of the Church today – especially in Europe. 'Many Europeans today think they know what Christianity is, yet they do not really know it at all . . . Many of the baptized live as if Christ did not exist' (*EE* 47). It is this, says Whitehead, that gives the impetus to the ecclesial movements. Also taking a lead from John Paul II's *Ecclesia in Europa*, Luis Fernando Figari, Javier Prades López and Kiko Argüello reflect on the social and cultural difficulties which beset the world so that today 'can seem a time of bewilderment. Many men and women seem disorientated, uncertain, without hope, and not a few Christians share these feelings' (*EE* 7). In response to these feelings, many of the writers offer their own diagnosis and solutions. Bryan Cunningham articulates a theory of attachment that emphasizes the importance of a sense of belonging – to others, to the world – and ultimately recognizing that belonging as belonging to God. Christine McGrievy in her essay on L'Arche reminds us that the weak and fragile are not simply objects of service but also teach and heal those who come to serve them; they also challenge contemporary culture: 'our culture lives on success and the values it engenders, and it cannot cope well with perceived failure'. Mario Marazziti from the Sant'Egidio community offers a vision of a community as a place and a means of reconciliation. López offers a careful reflection on how the sacramental life of the Church permeates all aspects of the life of the faithful. Kiko Argüello and François-Xavier Wallays invite us to take seriously the role and vocation of the family. There are many other insights and challenges for all readers, lay or ordained, active or contemplative, encouraged or dismayed by the Church and the world today.

Just as any healthy congregation will include a variety of people with different insights and experiences, and that would be not just expected but realized, so here. And similarly, just as that variety of insight and experience would be fruitful for reflection, so these essays offer us a great resource to explore

the life of the Church today and its task of mission and evangelization through different perspectives. As Paul reminds his
hearers in the First Letter to the Corinthians (1 Cor. 12.12–
21), the Church is the Body of Christ formed of many members, all different, but all with their purpose. So in the Church
today, the ecclesial movements are discovering their place and
their role. It is clear that in Pope John Paul these movements
have a champion who urges the whole Church to embrace
their insights and experiences:

> The movements and new communities, providential
> expressions of the new springtime brought forth by the
> Spirit with the Second Vatican Council, announce the
> power of God's love which in overcoming divisions and bar-
> riers of every kind, renews the face of the earth to build the
> civilization of love. (Pentecost Sunday 1998)

Finally, a suggestion on how to read these essays. The tempta-
tion when faced with a collection of different entities is to compare and contrast, to look for differences and similarities in
structure and action. This would be a natural but unhelpful
way of approaching this particular collection. The essay by
Charles Whitehead helps us get our bearings among the
ecclesial movements, but the rest are all very different in
style, content and purpose. Furthermore, there is a danger in
asking the question, 'Yes but what do they do?' about these
movements. It is perhaps instinctive to try to focus on the
specific activity of the members of the various ecclesial movements. In some cases this would be very simple – the L'Arche
community, we could say, was about working with people with
disabilities. But this would not do justice to the vision of that
community, and such an approach would frustrate us in
exploring many of the other movements where a specific activity or way of being would be hard to find. We are well used to
the distinction between 'doing' and 'being' and that needs to
be acknowledged here. When we ask 'What is a Christian?'
we answer not in terms of what such a person *does* – prays,
helps others, believes certain things – but in terms of being
baptized, of being a disciple of Jesus Christ. The doing, the

activity, is a consequence of that (under the grace of the Holy Spirit). What is clear from many of these lectures, and implicit in the rest, is that what the different ecclesial movements offer is a way of being a Christian today. That is why, when reading these essays, I suggest that the most helpful approach is not to try to analyse the specific distinctions or categorize similarities but simply to allow the author to use the insights and experience of each movement to paint a vision of how that particular perspective can help the task of Christian living today. The ecclesial movements – like all members of the Body of Christ – are there for the benefit of the whole body; these lectures show something of what the movements are offering to the wider Church as it seeks to carry out its perennial task of mission and evangelization.

The following movements contributed to this book:

International Catholic Charismatic Renewal Services

The Catholic Charismatic Renewal is not a single, unified worldwide movement like many others. It does not have a single founder or group of founders. It is a highly diverse collection of individuals, groups, services and activities, often quite independent of one another, in different stages and modes of development and with differing emphases, that nevertheless share the same fundamental experience and espouse the same general goals. These patterns of loose-knit relationships are found at local, diocesan and national levels, as well as on the international level. These relationships are very often characterized by free association, dialogue and collaboration rather than by integration into an ordered structure. The central goals of Catholic Charismatic Renewal include fostering a decisive personal receptivity to the person, presence and power of the Holy Spirit, and the reception and use of the spiritual gifts (*charismata*) for the benefit of the whole Church.

These and other central goals, with the projects that flow from them, have marked the Catholic Charismatic Renewal in individuals, prayer groups, communities, local, diocesan and national service teams and ministries since its beginnings in 1967. In order to serve the needs for cooperation, communication and coordination, a council and an international office were set up in 1978 under the auspices of Leon Joseph Cardinal Suenens, named by Pope Paul VI as his Episcopal Adviser to the Charismatic Renewal on the international level. The council was formed of leaders from around the world, and the office was first established in Brussels and later in Vatican premises in Rome. Since 1978 the council has developed an international organization which on the one hand promotes communication and cooperation among worldwide national renewal organizations, and on the other hand provides a channel of communication and cooperation for the international renewal with the Holy See. This Rome-based organization is called ICCRS (International Catholic Charismatic Renewal Services) and serves an estimated 120 million Catholic charismatics worldwide.

ICCRS consists of an international council which establishes the central goals, objectives and projects, and carries them out through its office in Rome. ICCRS is a juridical personality *'ad instar'*, corresponding to a private association of the faithful, and received its statutes from the Holy See in 1993. It is at the worldwide level the principal coordinating organization of the Catholic Charismatic Renewal (CCR), with a mission to serve and promote the CCR all over the world, under the Holy Spirit's action, in close contact with the Holy See through the Pontifical Council for the Laity.

The Community of Sant'Egidio

The Community of Sant'Egidio began in Rome in 1968 when a group of high school students gathered to consider how to change the world through the Gospel. Today, it is a movement embracing 40,000 Christian laypeople in more than 60 countries throughout the world committed to prayer, solidarity, friendship with the poor, peace, ecumenism and interreligious dialogue.

The services of each community foster intimate friendships with the poor hidden away in the cities. The community's border-dissolving charisma has led to work in peacekeeping and mediation in conflicts worldwide, as well as a campaign against the death-penalty, and a nationwide AIDS treatment programme in Mozambique. The community also organizes the world's largest annual interfaith meetings: a task entrusted to it by the Pope, following the world prayer for peace in Assisi in 1986.

The Vatican has officially recognized the Community of Sant'Egidio as a public lay association.

The Community of the Beatitudes

The Community of the Beatitudes was founded in France in 1973 by Ephraïm and Josette Croissant and another young couple, Jean-Marc and Mireille Hammel. In deepening their sense of the Jewish roots of Christianity and inspired by the paradox of power and weakness imaged in Jesus (cf. Rev. 5.5–6) they chose the name *Communauté du Lion de Juda et de l'Agneau Immolé* which literally translates as 'Community of the Lions of Judah and of the Lamb that was Slain'. Some years later, in order to demonstrate its commitment to the poor and to facilitate wider inculturation, the name was changed to *Communauté des Béatitudes* – 'Community of the Beatitudes'.

From an early stage, the community attracted members from different canonical states of life. Lay people – single and married, seminarians, nuns and priests, all united as the people of God, one in the calling to imitate the first Christians in a sharing of life and faith (Acts 2.42–47). The heart of the community is liturgical and deeply contemplative yet sharing of goods through the practice of hospitality and almsgiving is also pre-eminent. The community is hallmarked by fervent Eucharistic devotion and a deep love for the Blessed Virgin yet they retain a genuine ecumenical openness and an enduring concern in prayer for the peoples of the Holy Land. Likewise, the remarkable and radical nature of the *Communauté* has not constrained the charism, and there are now member groups in some 35 countries on five continents.

Communion and Liberation

Communione e Liberazione is a movement which originated in Milan during the 1950s. Fr. Luigi Giussani, convinced by John's Prologue that the origin and true destiny of humanity is to be found in Christ, began to explore new ways of sharing this mystery in the Berchat High School among a group that became known as *Gioventù Studentesca* – 'Student Youth'. Through praying together, public cultural debates, charitable activities, retreats, sporting activities and theatre visits, *Gioventù Studentesca* had a vivacious dynamism. Its activities and membership spread beyond the bounds of the city and soon the network of affiliated groups had reached all parts of Italy and beyond. The pivotal convulsion in student culture in 1968 caused a degree of heart-searching in *Gioventù Studentesca*. What emerged in 1969 was a movement with a new name, *Communione e Liberazione*. This literally translates as 'Communion and Liberation' but it is necessary to add the resonance of 'love and freedom' to capture its essence. *Communione e Liberazione* emphasized the unique revelation of Christianity as *the* New Fact of History calling us to communion with one another so that we might find authentic liberation.

Communione e Liberazione is present in some 70 countries around the world. Belonging is not by list or qualification but rather the free participation in community activities by members. The weekly gatherings in the 'School of Community' serve, as the name implies, catechesis and fellowship. Members are also nourished by the monthly magazine, *Traces – Litterae Communionis. Communione e Liberazione* seeks to foster fullness of life (John 10.10) by a lively questioning of our life and purpose in dialogue with Catholic tradition and encounter with Christ. It is in commitment to Christ that we find ourselves, our true belonging and our true freedom.

Schönstatt

Started in 1914 in the small village on the Rhine of the same name, Schönstatt was rooted in the religious life and work of its founder, and was to develop as a lay-movement of renewal within the Church. Its point of departure is the Marian shrine, which forms the heart of the movement.

During the interwar period (1918–38) Schönstatt was to develop as a Church movement. As such, it belongs to the first of these movments which sprung up in the last century. Its founder, Fr. Josef Kentenich, was very much aware of the dramatic changes in the world and society, and sought to find ways to respond so that the Church would be able to communicate with the emerging world in all its complexities. Thus Schönstatt was not developed around a conference table but was born out of the needs of the times. In the 1960s Fr. Kentenich explained: 'To a certain extent we can say that Schönstatt developed to meet and help develop the pastoral aims of the Second Vatican Council.'

As such Schönstatt sought to become a school of applied spirituality seeking to help people to grow as Christians in the modern world. With time, it developed a three-dimensional spirituality, the heart of which is covenant spirituality centred on personal relationship in the natural and supernatural framework. Everyday sanctity, an application of the covenant in ordinary life, strives to live in the context of Gospel values, finding harmony among attachments to God, humanity and creation – particularly inspiring the world of work and society, so that living in the world can be a way to God. The third dimension is a spiritual attitude of being an instrument in the building of God's kingdom: instrumentality. This aspect concerns itself directly and indirectly with the tasks of evangelization.

In the meantime, Schönstatt has grown to become an international movement. Based on the network of over 200 centres in 29 countries across the continents, the movement works in small groups: family groups for married couples, mothers' groups, women's groups, men's groups and youth groups for boys and girls. The strongest group at the present time is the family branch. There are five Schönstatt secular institutes and an institute for families, which serve the development of the movement in the service of the Church.

L'Arche

> 'In a divided world, L'Arche wants to be a sign of hope. Its communities, founded on covenant relationships between people of differing intellectual capacity, social origin, religion and culture, seek to be a sign of unity, faithfulness and reconciliation.' (L'Arche Charter, 1.4)

Jean Vanier founded L'Arche, having spent eight years in the British Navy and several more teaching philosophy in Toronto. His friendship with Father Thomas, a French Dominican priest, brought him into contact with people with learning disabilities and opened up for him St Paul's words: 'but God chose what is foolish in the world to shame the wise; God chose what is weak in the world to shame the strong; God chose what is low and despised in the world, things that are not' (1 Cor. 1.27).

Jean Vanier became deeply touched by the simplicity of the people with learning disabilities, their welcome and their pressing call to form relationships, and in 1964 he answered God's call and started to share his daily life with Raphael Simi and Philippe Seux. They lived in a small house in Trosly-Breuil in the north of France and named their home L'Arche.

From these very modest beginnings other communities were founded, first in Toronto, then another in Cognac, and a further community in Bangalore. Today, the international federation of L'Arche numbers 124 communities in 30 different countries, existing in very diverse religious, cultural and economic contexts. 'These communities, called into being by God, are united by the same vision and the same spirit of welcome, of sharing and simplicity' (L'Arche Charter, Introduction). All L'Arche communities are communities of people with learning disabilities and those who are called 'assistants', who choose to come to live and to work, to celebrate and to pray with them. Some of these 'assistants' are single, others are married; some stay for a few months or a few years and then move on; others discover that God is calling them to live L'Arche as a long-term vocation.

L'Arche communities are open and desire to form an integral part of life in their localities, seeking to foster relationships with neighbours and friends. Members are integrated with local churches or other places of worship.

Members of all L'Arche communities are called to live in solidarity at home and throughout the international federation.

Neocatechumenate Way

The Neocatechumenate as a movement developed in Spain in the 1960s in response to the call of the Church to renew herself in the wake of the Second Vatican Council. Its two founders were Francisco Argüello (better known as Kiko) and Carmen Hernandez. Their work began in the shantytown of Palomeras Atlas in Madrid, with the conviction of Christ's presence among the poor, and inspired by the life and work of early twentieth century hermit Charles de Foucauld. The 'way' of the movement is to gather in communities and create a grassroots network for evangelization. For the Neocatechumenate their 'way' is a return to the first Christian communities, the 'way' or journey is a rediscovery of baptism, similar to the catechumenate of the early Church. These communities work in the parishes to promote a 'tripod' basis of catechesis: Word, Liturgy, and Community.

For the movement, the Word implies the proclaiming of the Gospel (*Kerygma*) anywhere and everywhere; the Liturgy represents the celebration of Faith, within which all the symbols of tradition are remembered; and the community (*Koinonia*) denotes the communion between those who have heard the Word and live in the unity of love in the power of the crucified Christ.

There are now some 13,500 communities in 4,000 parishes and 650 dioceses in more than 90 countries.

Sodalitium Cristianae Vitae and Christian Life movement

The Sodalitium Christianae Vitae was founded in Lima, Peru, on 8 December 1971 by Luis Fernando Figari. The members of Sodalitium, laymen and clergy, consecrate their lives to the apostolate and live in community. As part of the universal evangelizing mission of the Church, the Sodalitium members have, as priority areas of the evangelizing service, the apostolate with the youth, the solidarious charity for the poor, the evangelization of culture and the apostolate with families.

In 1985 Figari founded the Christian Life Movement, which received approval from the Holy See in 1994 as an international movement of the faithful. The union of the diverse institutions that share the Sodalit spirituality form the Sodalit Family, that extends to more than 22 countries in America, Europe and Asia.

The Focolare movement

Chiara Lubich, the founder of Focolare, was born on 22 January 1920 in Trent, a city in northern Italy. It is best known for the famous Council of Trent that assembled to debate the challenge presented to the Catholic Church by the Protestant Reformation. Therefore, it seems highly significant that from this city, which witnessed the fracture among believers, 400 years later the 'Focolare', a movement for unity, should originate.

It began in 1943, during the Second World War and the heavy bombing of Trent. Chiara and her friends wondered if there was an ideal that no bomb could ever take away from them, and they concluded that an indestructible ideal did exist – God. They decided to make him the ideal of their lives. In practical terms they understood that the way to love God was to try to do his will by translating his word into their daily lives. For example, 'whatever you do to the least you do to me' they discovered meant loving those around them in a practical way by sharing the little they had, or accompanying someone elderly or with children to the air raid shelter, even at risk of their own lives. Each time they came together, they would share their experiences of living the Gospel in this way. In fact, people felt such spiritual warmth in their company that they gave them the nickname 'Focolare', which means hearth or fireplace. In the space of a few months, there was a community of 500 people living in a similar way.

The charism that the Focolare movement stresses is unity, and its spirituality is often referred to as the 'spirituality of unity' or communion. Those who live this spirituality discover a particular sensitivity to unity, which embraces people of all races and cultures. The Focolare movement has now developed in 182 countries, involving Christians of different churches, people of other religions and many others without any formal faith. People have found that this spirituality has much to contribute to the fields of politics, art, science, economy – indeed to every aspect of humanity – and this has been recognized in the many honorary degrees awarded to Chiara in different countries. Various awards – among them the Templeton Prize for Progress in Religion in 1977 and the UNESCO Prize for Peace Education in 1996 – have expressed appreciation of her work for unity and universal fraternity.

1

The Role of the Ecclesial Movements and New Communities in the Life of the Church

Charles Whitehead

It is very common to hear the ecclesial movements referred to as lay movements – no doubt because the majority of their members are lay people. But the new movements contain bishops, clergy and religious as well as lay people. They are for the whole Church. Some lay people are so committed that they take on a consecrated life through vows of chastity, poverty and obedience, and thereby become almost religious. Whilst the movements and new communities are a rich source of vocations to the diocesan priesthood, it is also the case that in some countries priests are being ordained for ministry in particular movements and communities.

So I would suggest that the movements and new communities are truly the Church, in the sense of the community of the baptized which we find in the New Testament and in *Lumen Gentium*, and therefore the description 'ecclesial movements' is more appropriate than 'lay movements'.

The Church usually looks upon and speaks about the ecclesial movements and the new communities together, so I will do the same. Some of the movements find expression in the form of communities, so at times there is some overlapping.

I would also like to mention at the outset three events which I believe are important landmarks in the history and development of the ecclesial movements and new communities: These are

1. The World Congress of Ecclesial Movements and New Communities, which took place in Rome at the invitation of the Pontifical Council for the Laity from 27 to 29 May 1998.

2. The meeting of Pope John Paul II with the ecclesial movements and the new communities, which took place on the
   eve of the feast of Pentecost on 30 May 1998, in the Piazza
   San Pietro, Rome.
3. The worldwide Bishops' Meeting in relation to the Ecclesial
   Movements and New Communities in the Church, which
   took place from 16 to 18 June 1999 in Rome.

I shall refer to these events during the course of this chapter.
All three are of considerable importance in the history of the
ecclesial movements and the new communities because they
demonstrate publicly the clear commitment of the Holy
Father himself, of the Congregation for the Doctrine of the
Faith through the participation of Cardinal Joseph Ratzinger
(now Pope Benedict XVI), and of the Pontifical Council for the
Laity (who organized the three gatherings).

In considering the role of the ecclesial movements and
communities I will attempt to answer five questions centring
around their identity, definition, origin, relationship with the
institutional Church and role in the life of the Church today. I
will begin with the question of identity.

1. Who (or what) are these ecclesial movements and new communities?

A conservative estimate would identify more than 200 lay
movements – many of them communities. Some are better
known than others; some are much larger than others. They
include: Ascent, Charismatic Renewal, Communion and Liberation, Cursillo, Focolare, L'Arche, the Neocatechumenal
communities, Sant'Egidio, Youth 2000, the Beatitudes community, the Chemin Neuf community, Opus Dei and many
more.

The movements and communities have much in common
but are also quite distinct, each with their own particular
charisms. They have different structures and operate in different ways. Most have a human founder, envisioned and
guided by the Holy Spirit. Many are ecumenical. All are con-

cerned with serving the community, and bringing a renewal of faith. They attract young people, and encourage vocations to the priesthood. Not all are happy to be called a 'movement', for good reasons which we will come to in a moment. So let's turn to another very basic question:

2. How do we define a 'Movement'? What exactly is it?

In his message to the 350 invited participants in the May 1998 World Congress of Ecclesial Movements and New Communities, Pope John Paul II explained a 'movement' in these words:

> The term is often used to refer to realities that differ among themselves, sometimes even by reason of their canonical structure. If, on the one hand, that structure certainly cannot exhaust or capture the wealth of forms produced by the life-giving creativity of Christ's Spirit, on the other it does indicate a concrete ecclesial reality with predominantly lay membership, a faith journey and a Christian witness which roots its own pedagogical method in a precise charism given to the person of the founder in specific circumstances and ways. The charism's own originality which gives life to a Movement neither claims nor can claim to add anything to the richness of the *depositum fidei*, safeguarded by the Church with profound fidelity. Nonetheless, it represents a powerful support, a moving and convincing reminder to live the Christian experience fully, with intelligence and creativity. Therein lies the basis for finding adequate responses to the challenges and needs of ever-changing times and historical circumstances.

At the World Congress of Ecclesial Movements and New Communities in May 1998, I heard Cardinal Ratzinger (now Pope Benedict XVI) remind us that at different times in the history of the Church there have been significant moves of the Holy Spirit which have brought change and new life into the Church. The Cardinal referred to the Franciscans in the thirteenth century as a good example of what constitutes a movement:

Movements generally derive their origin from a charismatic leader and take shape in concrete communities. Inspired by the life of their founder they attempt to live the Gospel anew, in its totality, and recognize the Church without hesitation as the ground of their life without which they could not exist.

So, typically, a movement will have:

- a charismatic founder
- a particular charism
- some form of ecclesial reality and expression
- a predominantly lay membership
- a radical commitment to the Gospel
- a form of teaching or training closely linked to its charism
- a specific focus and a commitment to bringing its own emphasis or understanding into the life of the Church.

Moreover, it will see itself as an integral part of the Church and be engaged in what can broadly be described as evangelization and mission.

As I said earlier, not all are happy to be described as a movement, and with good reason. The Catholic Charismatic Renewal, for example, has no human founder, no membership lists and no formal programmes of teaching and formation. It is a highly diverse collection of individuals, groups, ministries and activities, often quite independent of one another, in different stages of development and with differing emphases. Nevertheless, all share the same fundamental experience and have the same goals. In 1996 Cardinal Suenens wrote: 'To interpret the [Charismatic] Renewal as a "movement" among other movements is to misunderstand its nature; it is a movement of the Spirit offered to the entire Church and destined to rejuvenate every part of the Church's life.'

Opus Dei does not accept the description, 'movement'. It falls into the category of 'personal prelature', subject directly to the Pope himself. And there are others who claim not to fit the description 'movement'; nevertheless that is where the

Church usually chooses to include them, and so to debate the point further is of little value.

3. How have the ecclesial movements and the new communities come into being?

In answering this question, and in order to understand the place and the significance of the movements and new communities in the life of the Church today, we need to look at them in the light of the Second Vatican Council.

The most important part of the work of the Council is generally agreed to be the document on the constitution of the Church, *Lumen Gentium*. It is in this document that we find the essential teaching on the nature of the Church, with chapters on 'The Mystery of the Church', 'The People of God', 'The Church is Hierarchical' and 'The Laity'.

Right at the beginning of 'The Mystery of the Church' we are reminded that 'The Spirit dwells in the Church and in the hearts of the faithful, as in a temple' (41–1 echoing the teaching of Paul in 1 Cor. 3 and 6), and we then read that 'he bestows upon her varied hierarchic and charismatic gifts, and in this way directs her and adorns her with his fruit'.

Later, we are reminded that the Holy Spirit

> distributes special graces among the faithful of every rank. By these gifts he makes them fit and ready to undertake various tasks and offices for the renewal and building up of the Church. Whether these charisms be very remarkable or more simple and widely diffused, they are to be received with thanksgiving and consolation since they are fitting and useful for the needs of the Church. (2.12)

The institutional and charismatic dimensions of the life of the Church are not in opposition: both are essential to the well-being and life of the Church. *Both come from the Holy Spirit.*

In its first two chapters, *Lumen Gentium* does not divide the Church into lay and clerical members but sees her as the one Body of Christ. There are different functions and different gifts, bestowed by the one Spirit. It is clearly understood that the Church is hierarchical (and this is brought out more clearly in later chapters), but the definitions 'laity' and 'clergy' are expressed as 'the common priesthood of the faithful and the ministerial or hierarchical priesthood' which are 'ordered one to another; each in its own proper way sharing in the one priesthood of Christ' (2.10–11).

This is important because it reminds us that we all share in the sacraments of Christian initiation – baptism, confirmation and eucharist. So we are all initially simply Christians – the Church is made up of all the baptized, who all share the same Holy Spirit. Distinctions will come later. The hierarchical and the charismatic elements come from the *one source*, are in close association with each other and are *coessential* to the life of the Church.

It seems to me that this is an important understanding, brought to us by the institutional part of the Church, the Vatican Council, to prepare us for the establishment and development of the more charismatic parts of the Church – among them the new movements and communities, which emerged and developed in the late 1960s and 1970s.

This line of thought is developed more fully by Fr Ian Ker in his excellent CTS pamphlet *The New Movements – A Theological Introduction*, which has helped me to clarify my own thinking.

So my answer to the question, 'How have these movements and communities come into being?', is that they are clearly an initiative of the Holy Spirit, who has worked through the institutions of the Church to prepare for the arrival of the movements, and has also inspired men and women with particular visions of what is needed to strengthen and build up the Church in these times.

4. How do the ecclesial movements and new communities relate to the institutional Church?

Together, the ecclesial movements and new communities cover an enormous diversity of areas in the life and ministry of the Church: from works of mercy, through Christian initiation and catechetics, to social and political involvement and the new evangelization. Wherever they are found, they bring new life and enthusiasm into the Church, but sometimes cause tensions and difficulties, and are often misunderstood and rejected by many in the parish community.

I am well aware that any new endeavours, even those under divine influence, are not going to be greeted with positive reactions everywhere. Many mistakes have been made on both sides, and as the Holy Father said in addressing representatives of the movements and communities on 30 May 1998 'their unexpected newness ... has given rise to questions, uneasiness and tensions; at times it has led to presumptions and excesses on the one hand, and on the other to numerous prejudices and reservations'.

This has certainly been a period of testing for the movements and communities – testing their faithfulness and the authenticity of their charisms. But it has led, as the Pope puts it, to the challenge of a stage of 'ecclesial maturity'. This does not mean that all the problems have been solved, but it is clear that the movements and the institution are now travelling together, and that the journey is challenging for both!

Speaking to the worldwide bishops' meeting in Rome in June 1999 in relation to movements and communities in the Church, Pope John Paul asked the participating bishops to give pastoral priority to their care for, and guidance of, the movements and communities. He concluded his address to them with these words: 'Your great responsibility is not to impede the Spirit's gift, but, on the contrary, to make it bear even greater fruit in service to all Christian people.' He emphasized the importance of an ever stronger communion with the pastors whom God has chosen and consecrated, asking the bishops to reflect on how this special gift of the movements and communities could be welcomed in all its importance, in all its fullness and in all its dynamism.

At the World Congress of Ecclesial Movements and New Communities (May 1998), Cardinal Ratzinger (now Pope Benedict XVI) explained that 'the monastic movement created a new centre of life that did not abolish the local ecclesial structure of the post-apostolic Church (I understood him to mean the pastoral ministry of the episcopate, and the local clergy) but that neither did it simply coincide with it.' He linked the institutional and the charismatic dimensions by describing monasticism as 'a life-giving force, a kind of reservoir' from which the local Church could draw 'truly spiritual clergy' in whom the fusion of institution and charism was constantly renewed.

Pope Benedict XVI sees monasticism as one of the spiritual movements that has brought new life into the Church; he regards the ecclesial movements and new communities of our own times as the Holy Spirit clearly speaking to us once again, and again bringing us new life to meet the needs of today. In his view, the Church needs the energy, the witness and the service of the movements, and the movements need the guidance of the Church. He told us that the rise of new spiritual movements in the Church's history almost always makes someone uncomfortable, but usually that is a sign of the Holy Spirit at work. 'It is not correct', he said, 'to pretend that everything must plug into a uniform organization; better to have less organization and more Spirit.'

He told us that it is almost inevitable that the vivacity and totality of commitment made by members of movements will lead to tension between the community and the local parish. Finding a way to become part of the parish, to support the parish and draw support from it, is a spiritual challenge for the movement and the parish. At the same time, he said, pastors and bishops must recognize that they have no right to indulge in any claim of absolute uniformity in organization and pastoral planning. Bishops and priests cannot equate their own pastoral plans with the work of the Holy Spirit. 'It can happen that the Church makes herself impenetrable to the Spirit of God which gives her life,' he said.

While the Church is meant to be a communion, one cannot embrace a concept of communion in which the supreme pastoral value consists in avoiding conflict. In his own words: 'Faith is always also a sword and can require conflict for the love of truth and charity.'

At the 1998 meeting with the movements and new communities, John Paul II stated:

> I have often had occasion to stress that there is no conflict or opposition in the Church between the institutional dimension and the charismatic dimension, of which movements are a significant expression. Both are coessential to the divine constitution of the Church founded by Jesus, because they both help to make the mystery of Christ and his saving work present in the world. Together they aim at renewing in their own ways the self-awareness of the Church, which in a certain sense can be called a 'movement' herself, since she is the realization in time and space of the Father's sending of his Son in the power of the Holy Spirit.

So the ecclesial movements and new communities have received strong support, first from Pope Paul VI and even more from Pope John Paul II. But they are also often criticized at the local level for being elitist and divisive, and most Catholics know very little about them. This is hardly surprising. Any group that wishes to live a deeper spiritual life, that claims to have a particular vision to bring to the life of the local Church, and that wants to see its charisms accepted and used, is going to be seen as a challenge or threat by those who are by nature resistant to change. In our constantly changing world, many parishioners will resist the introduction in their local church of the challenge of anything that is new and different.

5. What is the principal role of the movements and new communities in the life of the Church?

Evangelization was not one of the major themes of the Second Vatican Council, but following Pope Paul VI's encyclical *Evangelii Nuntiandi* in 1974, Pope John Paul II always emphasized the need for a new evangelization. With the decline in church attendance in the Western world, it is now essential that the Church moves from a 'maintenance' to a 'missionary' mentality, and finds effective ways of presenting the Gospel to our secular society.

In *Ecclesia in Europa* (47) the Pope reminds us of the need for a renewed proclamation of the Gospel even for those already baptized. He writes:

> Many Europeans today think they know what Christianity is, yet they do not really know it at all. Often they are lacking in knowledge of the most basic elements and notions of the faith. Many of the baptized live as if Christ did not exist: the gestures and signs of faith are repeated, especially in devotional practices, but they fail to correspond to a real acceptance of the content of the faith and fidelity to the person of Jesus.

It is sadly true to say that in most European Catholic and mainstream Protestant parishes, numbers are falling rapidly. In contrast, the new movements and communities in the Catholic Church are showing remarkable growth both in Europe and worldwide – an experience paralleled by the expansion of the 'new' or 'house' or 'community' Protestant and Pentecostal churches. It is against this background that John Paul II called the historic World Congress of the Movements and Communities in May 1998 in Rome.

The Congress brought together 350 invited participants for reflection, sharing and discussion on the contribution of the movements and communities to the life and mission of the Church. Sixty movements and communities were represented at the Congress, with six cardinals, 28 bishops, and ten ecumenical observers.

There were three main aims of the meeting. It was to be

- a celebration of unity in diversity – many gifts but the same Spirit (1 Cor. 12.4)
- an opportunity to give thanks to the Holy Spirit for all the fruit evident in the lives of individuals and in the Church through the movements and communities
- a recognition of the fidelity of the movements and communities to the gifts they have received, and of their commitment to an even greater missionary responsibility.

The Congress, which was sponsored by the Pontifical Council for the Laity, was an important time of reflection and exchange on the theological nature of the movements and communities, and on their commitment to the new work of evangelization.

The first part was devoted to theological reflections which were begun by Pope Benedict XVI; the second covered the contributions of particular movements and communities to the mission of the Church; while the third was concerned with personal and practical experiences of the fruit born in the Church and in the world through the charisms of different movements.

The first part showed that the Church has accepted the movements and communities with their respective charisms, and has helped them fit into her structures. The second showed that the movements and communities have embraced an active role in the life and mission of the Church, and are playing their parts to the full with enthusiasm and vigour; while the third provided ample evidence from all over the world of the fruit of the work of the Holy Spirit in and through the movements and communities. Testimony after testimony referred to changed lives and transformed situations.

When it comes to changed lives, my own faith story is fairly typical, so I will outline it here.

I was brought up a Catholic, educated by the Jesuits. At school I was good at religious doctrine and the apologetics we were taught. When I went to university I had a very good intellectual knowledge of my Catholic faith, but soon found that it did not help me very much in my day-to-day life and I lapsed from the Church. It was 12 years later that my wife Sue and I met some Christians from a number of different churches who had a living faith which affected every part of their lives. For the first time I realized that what was missing for me was that personal, living relationship with Jesus Christ which lies at the heart of the Gospel message. As I entered into this living relationship with Jesus and the Father in the power of the Holy Spirit, everything I had been taught by the Jesuits fell into place, and my Catholic Christian faith became the most important thing in my life. My whole life changed, and I was aware of new priorities, a new sense of purpose and a new power in my life. This is the experience of many in the new movements and communities. One way of describing it would be to say that in my early life I had been catechized but not evangelized.

Immediately after the World Congress of Movements and New Communities another remarkable event look place. This was the meeting of the Holy Father with members of the ecclesial movements and new communities whom he had personally invited to Rome. This took place in the piazza San Pietro on 30 May 1998. The crowds filled not only the piazza and the via della Conciliazione, but also many of the side-streets leading into the piazza. Estimates of the number present vary from 350,000 to 500,000, and we need to remember that they were representing millions more all over the world.

As the Pope remarked, this was an unprecedented event, and it was my privilege not only to be there but to make a short speech of thanks on behalf of all the movements and communities represented.

The papal message was clear. In giving his personal endorsement and benediction to the 60 movements and communities represented, John Paul II called us to 'ecclesial maturity', to closer communion with the Church and especially with our local bishops, and sent us out as the front-line forces in the new evangelization.

When he spoke of the role of the movements and communities, he did so in these words:

> Today, to all of you here and to all Christians, I want to cry out 'Be open and docile to the gifts of the Spirit! Accept with gratitude and obedience the charisms that the Spirit never ceases to bestow . . . given for the common good, that is, for the benefit of the whole Church! . . . In our world, often dominated by a secularized culture which foments and advertises models of life without God, the faith of many people is put to a hard test and not rarely suffocated and stifled. In this context, there is clearly an urgent need for a strong

proclamation and solid, indepth Christian formation. What a need there is for mature Christian personalities who are aware of their own baptismal dignity, of their own vocation and mission in the Church and in the world! What a need there is for living Christian communities! Here then are the movements and the new communities: they are the response, stirred up by the Holy Spirit, to answer this critical challenge at the end of the millennium. You are this providential response!

He concluded with this prayer:

Come Holy Spirit and make the charisms you have bestowed ever more fruitful. Give new strength and missionary zeal to these sons and daughters of yours who are gathered here. Enlarge their hearts, enliven their Christian commitment in the world. Make them courageous messengers of the Gospel, witnesses of the risen Jesus Christ, Redeemer and Saviour of humankind. Strengthen their love and faithfulness to the Church.

I would like to conclude by making a personal comment on the relationship between the ecclesial movements and new communities and life in a normal parish.

Like many Catholics, I am committed to my parish and active in many parts of its life. I belong to a very good and active parish. We have over 50 organizations working in the parish in partnership with our priests. But if I am really honest, much of parish life still falls below my hopes and expectations. Our liturgies could often be better, and our corporate prayer life leaves much to be desired. There is a limited sense of community, and the new evangelization is something with which we struggle. I suppose that what is offered in our parishes is aimed at satisfying the expectations of an average parishioner, rather than at those who want to live a much richer experience of their faith.

So it's often the case that members of the movements and communities who want to live a fuller Christian life are seen as overzealous and superspiritual by the majority of parishioners, and even by many parish priests. Our presence in a parish is often seen as unhelpful, for reasons I have suggested earlier.

I am among the first to acknowledge that members of movements and communities have often made mistakes in their attitudes to other parishioners, in their behaviour and in their unrealistic expectations of parish life. We have often given an impression of being elitist, looking upon others as in some way sub-Christians. But it must also be recognized that our commitment to Christ and our missionary zeal are desperately needed, and this is where we have a vital contribution to make.

The movements and communities have been born of the Spirit to meet some very specific needs. Broadly speaking, we may list these as:

- the need for a deeper spirituality, which parishes can rarely offer
- the need to be more active in evangelization, particularly in the worlds of economics, politics, media, the professions and education
- the need to reinforce Christian values in marriage and family life
- the need to build community through a commitment to fostering community life in the parish
- the need to help with the sacraments of initiation, with post-baptismal catechesis and Christian discipleship.

In Pope John Paul II's words: 'Many of the baptized live as if Christ did not exist: the gestures and signs of faith are repeated, especially in devotional practices, but they fail to correspond to a real acceptance of the content of the faith and fidelity to the person of Jesus' (*EE*, 47). The movements and communities are ideally placed to address these problems.

I believe that the call to the ecclesial movements and new communities is to work humbly in all of these areas at parish and at diocesan level, in the power of the Holy Spirit, in service of the Church and to extend the Kingdom of God in our midst.

Many years ago I came across a similar hope, expressed in rather different language, on a Pentecostal church hoarding:

If all the sleeping people will wake up
If all the lukewarm people will fire up
If all the crooked people will straighten up
If all the depressed people will cheer up
If all the estranged people will make up
If all the gossiping people will shut up
If all the dry bones will shake up
If all the true believers will stand up
If all the church members will show up
To honour Him who was lifted up . . . then we'll have the world's greatest renewal in our church and in our town to the glory of God!

I commend the thought to you.

2

'A Church that Is and Works to be a Church for Everyone, but Particularly the Poor' (*Pope John XXIII*)

Mario Marazziti and Austen Ivereigh

Like many of the remarks of Pope John XXIII, the vision of the Church he set out on the eve of the Second Vatican Council was not entirely grammatical, but it was profound. The early Christian community would have recognized that vision: a Church where everyone is welcome, but where a primary place is given to the unfortunate of society: a community gathered, in other words, to embrace the widow, the orphan and the stranger.

There is no movement of lay people in the Church which better understands this vision than the community of Sant' Egidio. It goes back to the early 1970s, when a group of students used to gather in Rome's bohemian Trastevere district. Ten of them had been at school together at the Virgilio Lyceum in 1968, when social revolution was in the air. They, too, wanted to change the world, but through a radical living-out of the Gospel. At the edge of their vision was Pasolini's Rome of shanties filling with southern migrants. After school they headed there on their Vespas, became friends with families, ran 'popular schools' for children, built houses and fed people. At night they roomed in basements in Trastevere to establish solidarity with the immigrants, the unemployed, the elderly and the lonely. Every day they prayed together, meeting in churches to read the Gospel – an act which, despite the Second Vatican Council, was still regarded by many priests as Protestant.[1] Piazza Sant'Egidio became a meeting-place, a place for discussion of what it meant to be a church present among – and hearing the Good News from – the poor. They asked:

'How can we spend our lives for others? How can we overcome the loneliness of the modern city? How can we change the world?'

Between 1968 and 1973 the group was known simply as *la comunità*. Then they leased from the government what had before 1870 been a Carmelite convent in the piazza Sant' Egidio, and took their name from the Church attached to it. Sant'Egidio is an awkward name to pronounce in English – *sant edge-idyo* – and the saint himself ('Saint Gilles' in French, 'St Giles' in English) is not especially famous. But his portrait in the church expresses much of the essence of the community. It shows a monk protecting a doe with his hand, which has been pierced by an arrow; at a distance is a prince holding the bow from which the arrow has come. The community takes its name, in other words, from a man who protects the weak from the strong: a man of the Word of God, and a man whose life is dedicated to prayer, community and hospitality. St Giles was also, in the universe of the time, a global figure, who came from Thessalonika in the East but died in France. And he even manages to be ecumenical, a monk of the undivided Church that is both Western and Eastern. All these are characteristics of the community of Sant'Egidio.

It is easy to forget how, between the third and seventh centuries, ordinary men and women took to monastic life in order to be like the apostles and change the world. In the West, it was an experience intimately bound up with exposure to the Word of God through the continuous absorption of Scripture, especially the psalms. The monks lived by the work of their own hands, offered hospitality to strangers and were assigned places in the choir, not according to their social rank or their clerical status, but according to their seniority in the community. They were, like St Benedict himself, lay people.

Members of Sant'Egidio – which now number several thousand in Rome and several thousand more in cities across the world – are, like the monks of that time, unpretentious, preferring to be small with the small. The community is prophetic, yet ordinary; humble, yet ambitious for peace; firmly anchored in the Gospel, but open to all. Almost all of its

40,000 members in 60 countries are lay people with jobs and families who put prayer and friendship with the poor at the centre of their lives. If they are people of education and privilege, they choose less demanding jobs in order to be more available for prayer and friendship.

No one can say how, exactly, a person becomes a part of the community: there are no vows or formal hierarchies as such. 'Whoever wants to come takes a step toward the community, which accepts him or her,' notes the founder, Andrea Riccardi. Joining, he says, is 'the result of two wills coming together'.[2] Riccardi acts as an abbatial figure and each of the local communities has a *responsible*, but the institutional structures are slight. The community now has a bishop – Vincenzo Paglia of the diocese of Terni, north of Rome – and a few priests. But they were all lay members of the community first.

Historically, therefore, the community identifies with that strand in the Church which ties St Benedict of Nursia to St Francis of Assisi – lay men and women whose intense relationship with the crucified and risen Jesus was shown in their relationship with the poor and their reading of Scriptures *sine glossa*. The community's work in reconciliation has its echo in St Francis's taming of the wolf of Gubbio and in his crossing the Mediterranean at the height of the Crusades to seek dialogue with the Sultan Melk-el-Kamal.

Cardinal Carlo Maria Martini, the former Archbishop of Milan and an old friend of the community, recalls wandering the streets of Trastevere in the early 1970s. A Jesuit priest at the time, he was troubled by the division immediately after the Second Vatican Council between, on the one hand, those who favoured commitment to the poor and the transformation of society, and those who, on the other hand, put their emphasis on spiritual growth and prayer. There must be some way, he thought, that these two could be brought together. Later he met some members of the community who invited him to come and see them.

Then I began to understand [he would later write], to appreciate this living synthesis of the primacy of God, of prayer, and of listening to the Word; of taking God's Word seriously and, at the same time, of dedicating oneself in a concrete, effective way to the poor; of studying society and its problems attentively and with discernment. What happened to me has surely happened to many others in much the same way, whether they later joined the community of Sant'Egidio, or became friends of it in many different ways, as occurred with Paul, Aquilla and Priscilla.[3]

The community was unmistakeably a child of the Second Vatican Council, with its talk of the 'the priesthood of the laity' and its call for Christians to return to the Scriptures. The year the students first met – 1968 – was also the time of student activism, of optimism, of revolution. Young people wanted to change the world.

So too did the community. But while it shared something of the 'spirit of 1968', the Sant'Egidio young people made a deliberate choice in favour of the Scriptures rather than ideology, rejecting both the Marxism of the time and the neoliberal capitalism which came later.[4] Since 1989, some people might call this a 'postmodern' refutation of the metanarratives – liberalism, Marxism, fascism, secularism – which have characterized the modern project. But Riccardi, an historian by profession, prefers to describe it as an option for history over ideology. He was struck, he said, by a line in a Godard film – 'You have to move from existence to history.' History, the theologian Yves Congar told Riccardi, creates a profound sense of reality: it teaches complexity; it creates memory. The Bible is, in this sense, history.

Sant'Egidio rejected, in other words, the dichotomy of student radicalism between pure thought and pure action. Sant'Egidio's path was the classic Christian radical one of contemplation in action. The divisions in the Church of the 1970s which bothered Martini – the false choice between, on the one hand, struggling for the Kingdom (which implied an option for left-wing politics) or, on the other, a refuge in spirituality, a concentration on interiority, which downplayed engagement with human structures – were not, therefore, the community's.

Sant'Egidio took to its heart the famous words of Karl Barth, that Christians should live 'with the Bible in one hand and newspapers in the other'.

Sant'Egidio has also spurned the old divisions of the high Middle Ages – divisions which persist in the culture of the modern Church – between 'spirituals' and 'carnals'. Spirituals were those who had the task and the privilege of attending to the things of God, while the carnals were to busy themselves with the things of this world. The word 'laity' comes from the Greek *laos*, meaning 'the people'; the word does not refer to a particular kind of people but traditionally signified what they were not – not monastic or clerical. To be lay was to be 'lower', to be concerned with earthly rather than spiritual matters.

Like the Second Vatican Council, the community rejected this distinction, opting for an incarnate spirituality. Yet in many ways it is a definitely lay spirituality – one which looked at society, as the Gospels do, from the point of view of the poor and the victim, but never allowing the poor to become a category. Martini wrote that Sant'Egidio was 'the Church beginning once again from its origins', whose spirituality was marked by its knowledge of the world of the marginalized. 'Their attention to the people who lived in the Roman slums explains their discovery of the themes, images, and sorrow which are proper to that reality – the cold of winter, the loneliness, the disease, the situation of women.'[5]

Most people come to know Sant'Egidio through two of Rome's most beautiful churches: the Basilica of Santa Maria in the main square of Trastevere, and the Church on Tiber island, San Bartolomeo all'Isola. Romans, and visitors, know that any night of the week, at 8.30 p.m., they will find in these churches a heart-soothing Vespers – known simply as *la preghiera*, 'the prayer' – sung by hundreds of young people. The prayer reminds visitors at first of Orthodox monastic office, with its smoky candles and icons, and choir and shimmering mosaics; but it includes at its heart a proclamation of the Gospel and a ten-minute reflection. Afterwards, the members of the community hang around the church or move into the square outside. Some will go off to eat in a little restaurant

the community owns, where the waiters have learning disabilities. Some will climb into a car to visit the homeless. Some
will go home to their families.

All this is, in a sense, the answer to the first question asked
by the students who gathered in 1968 at the Chiesa Nuova:
solitude – how to get out of it and discover others. What has
developed since then is the answer: prayer, fraternity and
friendship with the poor in an urban context. The contemporary city for the Community of Sant'Egidio is what the desert
was for St Antony of Egypt: on the surface a vast, unfriendly
place, where the individual is isolated, and must face his or
her devils. But it is also the place out of which Christian community, a glimpse of the Kingdom, can be born, through
prayer and friendship with the poor.

Who are the poor? Initially they were the slum children on
the outskirts of Rome. These days, they are the elderly, the
'new poor' of the Western city. They are also the immigrants,
the homeless, the disabled, the prisoners, the mentally ill, the
HIV-infected, the children with learning disabilities and the
gypsies – anyone, in short, who lives at the neglected margin
of the city and who appears, in the eyes of the world, to have
nothing to offer. But the community knows otherwise: to us,
the poor are the *anawim*, the favoured of God. They are where
we meet Christ. Our friendship with the poor is what nourishes us and protects us from the violence of self-assertion.

In the left-hand aisle of the Church of Sant'Egidio is a much-
loved wooden cross which was found, many years ago, by the
side of the road. It is, in fact, barely a cross at all, for it lacks
the cross-plank – the Jesus fastened to it is missing his arms.
But it symbolizes something important to the community:
it is our 'Christ without arms', the powerless Christ, the
Christ of weakness, the Christ of whom St Paul speaks
when he declares that he is at his strongest when he is at his
weakest. Christ-without-arms is also, for the community, its
method and means: the call to transform the world through
powerlessness.

Movements often have a charism which is unique to them –
a gift of the Holy Spirit. For Sant'Egidio, it is the charism of

reconciliation. The community's starting-place is always personal: it does not *work with* the poor; nor does it have an *outreach to* the poor. The community is *a friend to* the poor. It delights in meeting people who live on the other side of one of the city's numberless boundaries – between young and old, rich and poor, mobile and immobile – and forging a friendship. What springs from that friendship in terms of practical assistance depends, like all friendships, on what people need, and what can be given.

Whichever city they are in, the communities have a special relationship with its poorer parts. In Antwerp they work around the port areas; in San Salvador, the slums. In New York, as in London, the community looks out for the hidden poor: the elderly who live alone in high-rise blocks, attended to materially by social services but in human terms as abandoned as lepers in Calcutta. In Buenos Aires, the community's service is in La Boca, an area of the city where the destitute end up in houses on stilts to avoid the flooding river. In Havana, community members take the ferry across to Regla, where among the poor in the tin-shack houses they are greeted as good friends, friends to chat to, friends to offer mouth-burning home-made rum to. These friendships are very normal, as friendship always is. But what is extraordinary and quite abnormal is that the friendship exists between people who in contemporary urban society are separated by hidden chasms.

Riccardi speaks of the deception of the bourgeois city, the lie of prosperity, which can only be maintained by hiding away the poor. The community crosses the river, becomes friends to the friendless and unmasks that deception.

The community's high-profile work in peace-making is simply another expression of this border-dissolving charism. Sant'Egidio has a particular gift for the diplomacy of friendship, which has scored at least one famous success: the brokering of the peace agreement in Mozambique in 1994 which brought to an end the 16-year-long civil war in that country.[6] It was followed by a less successful but significant involvement in the Algerian crisis (1994–95), and a strong involvement in the Guatemalan peace accords of December 1996, which paved the way to a truth and reconciliation commission to look into crimes committed by the military regime of the 1980s. The work continues in many parts of the world: Lebanon, El Salvador, Colombia and, most recently, the Ivory Coast and the Sudan.[7] The community is in demand as a mediator because it has an extensive network of personal contacts, and credibility as an impartial negotiator without vested interests or ulterior motives.

The community's model for peace-making is the famous story of St Francis of Assisi taming the wolf of Gubbio. Like St Francis, the community comes to conflicts without any agenda or vested interest except peace with justice; like St Francis, they come unarmed, their weakness being their strength. Like St Francis, they start from the assumption that no one can be defined as so barbarian or evil as not to deserve even a word; and they embark on a dialogue which some regard – as the townspeople of Gubbio at first regarded Francis's dialogue with the wolf – as madness and possibly treason.[8]

Although the community became well known for its work in mediation, the new ventures also brought misunderstandings. It is not a kind of 'parallel Vatican diplomatic service' as it has sometimes been characterized.[9] When it began to be involved in conflicts, the community was not abandoning its work with the poor in favour of informal diplomacy, as some believed, but simply acting in response to its friendship with the poor. War is the mother of all poverty, and peace is above all necessary to the poor. When your friends are dying in a war, you try to end it. For the same reason, the community has set up in Mozambique Africa's first nationwide full AIDS treatment programme, and has argued that anti-retroviral treatment is a 'new human right' which must be extended to Africans.[10] If your friends in Mozambique are dying of AIDS, you want them to have the kind of anti-retroviral treatment your friends in Europe enjoy.

The community is also well-known in the Church for its networks of friendships within the Eastern Churches and between leaders of different faiths. After he gathered the world's religious leaders together in Assisi in 1986 to pray for peace, Pope John Paul II entrusted the community with continuing that task, which it does in enormous meetings of the world's faith leaders in different cities each year. The 'Religions and Peace' conference is one of the largest interreligious gatherings in the world. The 2003 meeting in Aachen (Aix-la-Chapelle), drew more than 500 religious leaders from 58 nations for a three-day session that ended with a joint appeal for peace. It was held in Warsaw for the 50th anniversary of the outbreak of the Second World War; in Jerusalem in 1995 for the first historic meeting of Jews, Muslims and Christians to discuss the future of the Holy Land; and more recently in Bucharest, where it contributed to a thaw in Catholic–Orthodox relations. In 2001, shortly before the 11 September attacks, the community brought together 20 cardinals, 11 patriarchs, seven Protestant bishops and an array of Jewish, Muslim and Buddhist leaders in an attempt to defy the pessimistic Huntingdon vision of the world as increasingly divided by conflict along religious lines.[11] After 11 September, the community organized an emergency Christian–Muslim summit in Rome to proclaim to the world that religion and violence were incompatible, and that the clash of civilizations now is no more inevitable than was the class struggle a hundred years ago.[12]

This has become a major theme of the community's public proclamations: that in a globalizing world which is bringing peoples of different cultures and religious beliefs closer together, humankind needs to develop a deeper capacity for dialogue and understanding. The alternative is to make the Huntingdon thesis plausible just as the Marxist thesis was plausible in an age of worker exploitation.

The community never forgets that Trastevere was once the place, in Roman times, where Jews and later Christians lived, outside the Aurelian wall; nor that, during the Second World War, the Jews in Trastevere were rounded up by German soldiers and sent to Auschwitz. What had made this possible was the herding in the Middle Ages of Jews into ghettos. As Rwanda, Bosnia and Northern Ireland show, proximity is no

guarantee of solidarity and peace. Which is why, every 16
October, the community organizes a candlelit march from
Trastevere to the old Jewish ghetto, tracing in reverse the
route taken by those 1,022 Jews (only four came back). The
community wants this moment remembered – lest Rome
forget.[13]

When he addressed the community some years ago, Pope
John Paul II singled out two of its vital characteristics:
filoxenia, its love of the outsider; and its openness to the universal.[14] The community tries to live 'without walls', conscious
of the tendency in both society and in the Church to build a
fortress around itself and to create scapegoats. To the tempta-
tion of the Church as refuge and the nation as fortress, the
community responds with a counter-logic of concern for the
one who is outside and far away. It refutes a false idea of peace
in which the East is regarded as fanatical and the Arab world
as fundamentalist, because it understands that these barriers
of the mind contain an inherent violence which can explode at
any time. The community has seen it too often around the
globe: in Rwanda, in Liberia and in Uganda.

The community has also raised its voice against the death-
penalty, creating a network of 5 million people who are calling
for an end to this obsolete, violent, ineffective, inhuman
instrument, just as Christians in the past called for an end to
slavery and torture.[15] On another issue, it rejects the notion
common in the North that AIDS in Africa can only be stopped
by prevention alone. The arguments against administering
full HAART anti-retroviral therapy to Africans are the same
arguments used against curing TB in the slums of Europe at
the beginning of the twentieth century. The arguments only
make sense if the poor are the distant other. Once we make
ourselves neighbours to them, the logic dissolves.

Visitors to Sant'Egidio's many projects in Rome are struck
by the way in which the poor are regarded as friends rather
than objects of compassion. Once a year, at Christmas, this is
vividly demonstrated when the pews in the Basilica of Santa
Maria in Trastevere are taken out and replaced by tables dec-
orated in seasonal reds and greens. From all over the city, the

poor come – the elderly, ex-prisoners, alcoholics, disabled, immigrants, homeless – to be served Christmas lunch. The same 'spirit of the Beatitudes' is visible any day of the week in the community's 'popular kitchen' in Trastevere, where 1,500 meals a day are served to the poor of Rome.[16]

Friendship with the poor is the means, for the community, of spiritual growth and redemption. The Western Christian tradition has always recognized that poverty and weakness are the terrain on which to leave behind the idolatries of this world. In our media-saturated cities, the idols are everywhere, exerting a fascination for us, tempting us to spend our money and time and energy on what fails to satisfy. Against these, the poor of our cities are our best defence; they recall us to the reality of our human dependence on others and on God.[17] The great emotional capacities of mentally ill people call into question the intellectual pride beneath the Western assumption that the complexity of the real world can be dominated by reason, just as physical handicaps are sobering for a society drunk on images of people as clean, beautiful and healthy. As Cardinal Camillo Ruini, on the community's 33rd anniversary in 2001, put it: 'To choose the poor is to choose God.'

Sant'Egidio's 'success', if it may paradoxically be called that, derives from its 'weak strength' – daily contact with the Word of God, and with the poor. It has become, as John XXIII said of the Church he envisioned, 'a village fountain', where rich and poor alike come to be cleansed of their diseases, their egotisms and their fears – a fountain, this time, for a global village.

In the Old Testament a city without walls is not a desirable place to be. It means allowing yourself to fall prey to your enemies. But in Zechariah, the city without walls is the fruit of the Pentecost. It is the place where the gates open to the outsider and peace flows within. It is the place of laughter and the love of friends, and the primacy of the poor. It is not a place which exists for itself, but for everyone; it does not belong, even, to the Community of Sant'Egidio. It is a gift: one that embodies a Church which is for everyone, but especially a Church for the poor.

Notes

1. I have memories of being thrown out every time from one place or another. The priest would eject us, saying 'You are not Catholics. You are Protestants. You read the Bible and there is no priest with you' (Riccardi, interview with Catherine Odell of the *National Catholic Register*, 20 February 2004).

2. Andrea Riccardi, *Sant'Egidio, Rome and the World* (St Pauls, 1996), p. 52. 'We have no formal commitment so no one would prevent me leaving tomorrow. Nevertheless, the community is extremely stable. It's not just an experience of one cycle of life. For me and for most of the others I know it has been choosing to live in a family' (Claudio Betti, interview with Margaret Coffey, Australian National Broadcasting Corporation 1999).

3. Cardinal Martini, Preface to Riccardi, *Sant'Egidio*. (St Pauls: London, 1996).

4. The Vatican correspondent of the *National Catholic Reporter* describes the community as being 'founded in 1968 by a group of young Catholic leftists who did not want to drift off into secular radicalism but remain anchored in the Gospel'. He adds: 'Sociologically and politically, the centre of gravity in Sant'Egidio is on the left, yet it has terrific contacts with the Vatican' (John Allen, *All the Pope's Men: The Inside Story of how the Vatican Really Thinks* [New York: Doubleday, 2004], p. 163).

5. See Preface to Riccardi, *Sant'Egidio*.

6. The peace negotiations lasted from 1990–93. The former Secretary-General of the United Nations, Boutros Boutros-Ghali, referred to the community's careful, painstaking method as 'the Roma formula'.

7. For more information, see website, www.santegidio.it

8. See Mario Marazziti, 'A Miracle of two fish', *The Tablet*, 28 September 2002, and Austen Ivereigh, 'What I saw in Assisi', *The Tablet*, 2 February 2002. For a detailed account of how the community brokered peace in Mozambique see Roberto Morozzo della Rocca, *Mozambique de la*

paix à la guerre. Histoire d'une méditation insolite (L'Harmattan: Paris, 1998).

9. 'The Vatican has never asked us. Each time we have acted as mediators in a conflict, whether in Mozambique, Algeria, Kosovo or Guatemala, we have chosen to. This doesn't mean that if the Pope asked us, we wouldn't. But he never has.' (Andrea Riccardi, interview with the Spanish newspaper *El Periódico*, 16 May 2001.)

10. See Austen Ivereigh, 'Time to treat AIDS in Africa', *The Tablet*, 15 December 2001. In May 2004 the community brought together the health ministers of 13 African countries in Rome to declare that Western-style AIDS therapy was a human right (*The Tablet*, 22 May 2004). The community pointed to their programme in Mozambique, where 97 per cent of children were born free of the AIDS virus, as proof that Africans do not have poor 'patient compliance'.

11. In *The Clash of Civilisations* (American Institute, Washington, DC, 1992), Samuel P. Huntingdon argued that the world was no longer divided by ideology but by religious fault-lines, and forecast growing tension.

12. See Austen Ivereigh, 'With Muslims in Rome' (*The Tablet*, 13 October 2001).

13. Andrea Riccardi believes that the founders' vision of the European Union as a network of deepening integration and solidarity has its roots in Auschwitz. He made the remarks at a meeting of the movements at Stuttgart. See Austen Ivereigh, 'Europe of the Heart' (*The Tablet*, 15 May 2004).

14. Riccardi recalls the community's first contact with Pope John Paul II in 1978:

> He was driving by our parish, the first parish he visited, and we called to him. He stopped and came in to visit the day care centre [for the elderly]. He sat on one of the little benches we had and said, 'Who are you?' We told him about the community and how we founded the centre. Two months later, he came back to visit the

whole community at the Church of Sant'Egidio. We think of him not so much as the Pope, but as the bishop of Rome – our bishop. (Odell, *National Catholic Reporter*, 20 February 2004.)

15. The community monitors progress towards the abolition of the death-penalty around the world at www.santegidio. org/en/pdm/index.htm. Whenever a death-sentence is commuted, the Coliseum in Rome is lit up.

16. The French newspaper *Le Nouvel Observateur* (30 October 2001) noted of the popular kitchen, that it was 'a place discreetly impregnated with the perfume of the Beatitudes: there the poor are invited to sit at a table and are served. They are treated with regard and delicateness, patiently being invited to renew their interactions in an atmosphere of peace and sweetness, where each one feels welcome and respected entirely as a person. In channelling their indignation at the scandal of evil through prayer, the members of Sant'Egidio escape the growls of revolts and imprecation and are impregnated with an evangelical invitation to deal with the effects of evil through the transformation of their own hearts.'

17. It's not natural to ask in prayer, because that calls for the adult to become a child, recognizing with faith his or her weakness and need. But the poor and the needy know how to ask (Riccardi, *Sant'Egidio*, p. 197).

3

Consecrated Families and the Community of the Beatitudes

François-Xavier Wallays

I am the moderator-general, that is to say, the leader on an international level, of a community comprised of around 30 houses in France, the country of its foundation, and around 30 houses outside of France spread over five continents. I shall start my account of our community by describing how its first members received their call.

History of the community

The community began on 25 May 1973, in a pizzeria in Montpellier, France, where the university students used to eat. The reason for the meal was to celebrate Josette's birthday (Josette was the young wife of our founder Ephraïm) and also the engagement of a young couple, Jean-Marc and Mireille Hammel.

A short time before this, all four had experienced what is known in the Charismatic Renewal as 'the baptism in the Holy Spirit'. This involves a personal encounter with the living, risen Christ in the Holy Spirit. As you know, this experience produces both a desire for conversion in those who receive it and the strength to enter into this process of conversion. Above all, it is accompanied by an awakening of the grace of confirmation, that is to say, the need to let oneself be constantly filled by the Holy Spirit, so that through us the Spirit can witness to Christ's resurrection, which also implies the desire to live every moment of one's life under the impulse of the Spirit (Gal. 6.8).

Like all new converts, Ephraïm, Josette, Jean-Marc and Mireille went through a kind of spiritual honeymoon with God, discovering his infinite mercy, his tenderness and his power, and, to quote the Curé d'Ars, 'the incredible privilege of being able to speak to him in prayer'.

And lo and behold! during the meal, somebody came out with the following: 'Suppose we lived together as a community?' It wasn't an idea or something sentimental, but rather the expression of something which was perfectly obvious: they experienced such a powerful communion among themselves that, of its very nature, it led to living and sharing together at a radical level. Was this enough to found a community? Of course not, but for several years the Lord had put the desire to found a community on Gérard Croissant's heart (Gérard was later to receive the name Ephraïm). To his way of thinking, it was the only way of being able to live the Gospel radically. He felt called to live in the same way as the first Christian community after Pentecost.

Founding charism – the consecration of marriage
For a community to exist and keep going there needs to be a person who bears the charism of founder. Brother Ephraïm was that person. However, for our community to come to birth a further step was needed: a step Ephraïm had taken several months before. In giving the sacrament of marriage to each other, Gérard and Josette decided to consecrate their union, their family, totally to God, and through this consecration, offer themselves to the Lord. Certain of having heard an interior call which was special to their union, they received the sacrament as a gift of God in response to their 'yes' to his calling. They were anointed at the very heart of their love for a mission. They knew it with that certainty which goes with the things of God. Without really understanding, they kept these things in their hearts.

If we go back to the time of the community's foundation in the pizzeria, we can see that for Jean-Marc and Mireille, saying 'yes' to living in community on the day they announced that they were getting married meant, in a veiled way, choosing to allow themselves to be dispossessed of their mutual love so that Christ would become the lord, guardian and source of this love. They agreed to say a 'yes' that they would have to continue to say daily as all the different dimensions of life and the call of God became known.

Our community was thus born of a gift given to a person, our founder, and of a couple's specific consecration, a consecration received within the consecration of the sacrament of marriage.

What kind of consecration?

How is it possible for a family to live in community? What kind of consecration does a couple live in the heart of the community?

The call of God

In community, the fundamental element enabling a common life of prayer, work and a sharing of material goods is the call of God. The new movements and communities are realities which convey grace for the whole Church because, through the power of the Spirit, they seek to incarnate the Gospel in the reality of today's world. Those who join the community and make a total gift of self respond to a call of the Holy Spirit. Of course, this call must be discerned and the person must consent to being transformed deeply and personally, so that the grace of this calling restructures the whole of their being. In the case of our community, the families and the first members to hear the call all witnessed to the fact that they were seized by the beauty of the world to come and by the certainty of Christ's imminent return in glory.

Our founder illustrates this experience by a short parable. When the Mont Blanc tunnel was under construction, the Italians and the French advanced blindly towards each other, each from their own side. As the work progressed, they started hearing the sound of the other team working opposite them on the other side. Just before the hole appeared between the two sides, there remained just a few yards of rock to clear before the two teams met up. At this point, both teams could hear one another and communicate. They were in the same tunnel, although separated by only a few yards of rock. This is the experience of the first community members, and it remains the living heritage into which all those who are called, or who will be called in time to come, must enter.

This is the reason why, during the first few years, all the brothers and sisters – single people and married couples alike – lived like monks. Nothing seemed more urgent for them than to contemplate the Kingdom to come in order to anticipate it and so proclaim it.

First dimension: contemplative life

In this way the contemplative dimension became inscribed in the heart of the community as a distinctive calling. The consecration of couples and single people in a life of contemplative prayer is thus a sign for everyone of the urgency of making our bodies and our relationships temples where God is praised and glorified. It is also a combat, which is perhaps more difficult for married couples than for single people because the former cannot use precisely the same means as the latter. Whilst living in community and desiring to be open to the contemplative dimension of their calling, because of their children and their specific mission, the couples must remain immersed in the world and not become separated from it.[1] They cannot hide behind the grill of an enclosed order so as to be concerned only with the things of God. But are they not part of a whole stream of consecrated life which aspires to live the contemplative life in the midst of the world, like Jesus of Nazareth? Is this not the challenge of the disciples of Charles de Foucauld, the little brothers and the little sisters of Jesus? Isn't this what the Eastern saints such as Seraphim of Sarov proclaimed when they prophesied a renewal of monasticism which would be lived out differently from life in the desert? This grace, destined to be given to those people who live a normal life in the world whilst being captivated by a gift of continual prayer, and who receive the joy of experiencing divine mercy as they repent tearfully for their sins, has been referred to as 'interiorized monasticism'.

Captivated by the Kingdom of God, and contemplating it, the first members received a new spirituality of which an essential element, the mystery of Israel, united us to our Protestant brothers who belonged to an association called the 'Union de prière de charmes'. This mystery is stressed by Saint Bernard and developed in France by Maritain, amongst others. It is a mystery which St Paul speaks about in his letter to the Romans and which concerns God's plan for Israel: a plan which will come about at the end of time. Our first foundation, after the mother-house at Cordes, was in Israel. From the very first week of community life, we united ourselves to the Jews around the world by celebrating a family-type liturgy on the Friday evening: a liturgy inspired by the Jewish prayer of welcoming the grace of Shabbat.

To unite oneself to the prayer of Israel, and contemplating the accomplishment of God's plans for Israel in Christ, gives us an idea of what is at stake regarding the Church's Jewish roots from an eschatological point of view. The consecration of a family which has a vocation of prayer can also receive much from the first covenant.

In Judaism, is not the father of a family the one who presides over the liturgy, and is not the family's identity received in listening lovingly to the Word of God and in seeking to be obedient to the Commandments?

The incarnation of the families' vocation in the community has had many different faces because all consecration deploys its vital momentum in a missionary dynamic.

Second dimension: community life
For the community members, anticipating the Kingdom of Heaven means to unite themselves through prayer and liturgical life with what is lived out in Heaven. The primary reason why they left everything was so as to be able to pray. But it was also, inextricably, through community life that they experienced the 'already here' of the Kingdom. In order to understand this, it is important to know that, in the world, the first members formed a network of friends. As the community came together, they experienced the fact that each one received a new place in the body of the community, different from the one they had had in the circles they belonged to

before. This place wasn't given according to their natural gifting or their past history, but was a new gift, a pure gift of the Lord's grace, given through the calling which he held out to them. Day after day, they experienced community as a gift of God which came down from Heaven, like the new Jerusalem in the Book of Revelation which is called to replace the city of Jerusalem.

The call of God opened their hearts to welcome a new reality – fraternal communion. A fundamental element was to nourish and strengthen this – the word of God. The Spirit of prophecy manifested itself in our midst right from the beginning through a particular gift – that of 'charismatically' receiving a word from the New Testament during the time of prayer which was given to enlighten and guide the community's path. This word, which is received in a very simple way (usually by opening the Bible in prayer), is most often accompanied by an exhortation given by the shepherd, actualizing the word received. It is through this that the brothers and sisters experience the fact of being known and loved by the Lord. How many times difficulties or even conflicts have been resolved by the word bringing to light secrets within the brothers' and sisters' hearts, most often without the one who is preaching even being aware of it. Allowing the cup of his heart to overflow, he doesn't realize the impact of what he is saying, ignorant of the inner struggles of those present. People from outside the community sometimes drive a long way just to come and share a time of prayer with us, because they need to be enlightened about something, knowing that the Lord will give them the word they can count on and from which they can draw peace of heart.

Third dimension: missionary activity
In one sense, a function of the consecration of families in the new movements and communities is to reveal the missionary identity of the domestic church which is the Christian family. For us, this has taken on different forms. Some families, either in their own country or abroad, have responded to the call to become pillars or leaders of new foundations, in great poverty

and in total abandonment to divine providence. In France, one family – both parents and children – prayed for eight years to be sent to found a house in America. We owe our presence in this country to them. Two families in which the husbands are both doctors – one a paediatrician, the other a neuropsychiatrist – left everything so that the community could run an abandoned hospital in the heart of Zaïre (now the Democratic Republic of Congo). Twenty-two years later, our brothers and sisters – some of whom have been there more than 20 years – are still serving the poorest of the poor, even though they have lived through three wars.

One couple whose children were already grown up worked first with the Apostolic Nuncio and then with a diocesan bishop for several years. They were replaced for a time by another couple, of which the husband had been an ambassador for his country. He had the opportunity of serving his old colleagues during receptions organized by the Nuncio and he lived out this experience as a witness to his attachment to Christ. This same couple spent many years travelling around several countries to evangelize children and parents by presenting a Christian puppet show. Another couple who didn't have children responded to a call to go from town to town organizing parish missions wherever it was asked of them.

For some families, their mission has been in the domain of their natural and professional abilities, whether welcoming those who suffer or are in difficulties, or through art, bookkeeping or teaching. But in order to exercise a natural talent in the Lord, one needs to have, in a certain sense, either lost the talent for a time or have given it back to God. Also, the first years of formation within the community are of utmost importance, as is becoming rooted in prayer.

A consecration which has a positive effect upon the children
We have also had the experience of a couple's consecration having a positive effect on their children, leading them in their turn to a consecration to God. The first 'member' of the community to enter into heaven was a child who had just been baptized. The fact of God calling the children of several com-

munity members to himself in this way has been a spiritually powerful event each time, although extremely painful.

It is rare for children of community members, once they become adults, to join the community. For them the community is a family, so they need to leave this family in order to become adult. They all remain marked by the radical nature and the coherence of their parents' choice of life, even if they are not always in agreement with it.

One thing which is often very precious to them is the place which we seek to give to the poor in the community. For example, they all know personally one or other of the 'homeless pilgrims of the road' whom we welcome for one or more nights, and who come back regularly or even decide to stay with us. To have been the friend of a 'poor person' as a child, is for some a priceless gift.

The fruits of the families' consecration

The specific vocations of consecrated persons
In the early days the community obviously attracted other families and a large number of people who wanted to get married, but it was also the place where single people were able to hear and respond to the call to be eunuchs for the Kingdom of God (cf. Matt. 19.12). If you will permit me to say so, this generated a new form of consecrated life in the Church. The community discovered itself to be the bearer of a new charism, whose novelty for the Church consisted precisely in the fact that it allowed for a communion of the different states of life all living the Gospel in the same radical way. In fact, consecrated brothers have been called to the priesthood and the community has become a 'communal home' made up of families, single people, consecrated brothers and sisters and priests. Moreover, in a certain sense, it is easier to discern, form and integrate single people who aspire to celibacy for the Kingdom of God in a community like ours than to do the same thing for a family, because the family is a veritable little community which has to be helped in each process of discernment. In addition, in the case of families, many things need to be

adjusted in different ways according to the social and cultural context. A spiritual tradition isn't formed in just a few days. Cenobitical life didn't happen overnight in Western or in Eastern countries, and the history of the mendicant orders shows how there is much trial and error before a new form of religious life in the Church can assume its definitive shape.

There is also the risk for the community that, being too fruitful in consecrated celibate vocations, it forgets its roots, becomes detached from them and develops into a classic religious congregation. However, through having consecrated members, the community calls forth vocations to the consecrated life and to priesthood, and feels responsible for attracting consecrated and priestly vocations for the Church.

The community has to deal – in the Lord – with what seems to be a contradiction: born out of the consecration of families and a place for families to be consecrated, the community, through its fruitfulness, could become a community of consecrated celibates. The response to this challenge implies seeking a better understanding of the gift that consecrated life and marriage are for each other. In order to illustrate this I would like to share a personal memory with you:

One day I was wishing a bishop a happy anniversary on the occasion of his silver jubilee as a priest, when he shared something with me which was making him suffer deeply: a big party had been organized for him, while his parents had had no celebration to mark their 50 years of sacramental marriage. And yet this was in Africa where Church marriages are rare. So he asked himself: in the face of African culture, which sees the religious leader as a being wielding supreme power, how would it be possible to make people realize the true identity of the pastor as the one who is configured to Christ, as the head, so as to be able to serve his brothers? How would it be possible to get everyone to see the splendour of our baptismal vocation and its cost? How could one incarnate the identity of the Church as the People of God, in Africa? This is what is at stake as regards our welcoming the work of the Holy Spirit in the Church today, and in particular for all the new movements and the new communities.

Suggestions for a deeper theological understanding

The new movements: a metamorphosis of the face of the Church
I wanted to begin my talk by telling the story of what God has done through the birth of the Community of the Beatitudes, in order to highlight the fact that the universal Church is living in a special time of grace where the Holy Spirit intervenes so as to do new things. It is a question of gifts which are given in order to respond to the specific needs of the men and women of our day, and of a movement for renewal in the Church, so that it can present the prophetic face which the world so needs today. As explained by Pope Benedict XVI (formerly Cardinal Ratzinger), at different times, the face of the Church has been turned upside down by the 'movements' that the Spirit has raised up within it. At the heart of these movements, there have often been one or more people who have a powerful charism. We can talk about there being a 'before' and an 'after' for the Desert Father, St Anthony, as there was for St Francis of Assisi and St Dominic. It seems that today we are seeing a metamorphosis of the visible traits of Christ's Spouse, accompanied by a deepening awareness of what makes up her identity. I would just like to point out a few elements.

The Church as a mystery of communion
The Second Vatican Council highlighted what most fundamentally characterizes the Church: the fact of it being a mystery of communion which is received from the communion of the Trinity. The Council affirmed the call of the baptized to holiness. This consists in uniting oneself to God, participating, through charity, in the infinite love of God. Everything in the Church is ordained to this purpose.

The Church's catholicity
Let's come back to the point that several new movements not only put an accent on the rediscovery of the Jewish roots of the Church, but also have the desire to see the place of Israel made manifest as being part of the Church's own mystery from an eschatological perspective. Through his trip to Jerusalem, and

more recently through his nomination of a bishop of Jewish origin for the community of Christians, Pope John Paul II lead us to entertain the possibility of the rebirth of a Jerusalem Church, composed of Christians of Jewish origin: a community which disappeared in the eleventh century. It is thus the mystery of the catholicity of the Church which takes on another form, because it is the affirmation that the Christian community cannot exist as a church other than in the mystery of the grace given to Israel. I am using this example, which is of tremendous consequence for the life of the Church, for her theology, for her spirituality, in order to show what is at stake in remodelling the face of the Church. The Second Vatican Council accentuated the concept of the people of God. At the same time this announced a gift of the Spirit to be received and also a work to be undertaken in order to incarnate the prophetic word received. The years following on from the Second Vatican Council have shown that it wasn't a question of beginning by putting new structures in place, or of redistributing authority, but rather of learning how to live the mystery of communion to a greater extent.

At the heart of ecclesial communion is communion of man and woman
In *Vita Consecrata* (1996)[2] paragraph 62 John Paul II declares:

> Worthy of praise are those forms of commitment which some married couples assume in certain associations and movements. They confirm, by means of a vow, the obligation of chastity proper to the married state and, without neglecting their duties towards their children, profess poverty and obedience. They do so with the intention of bringing their love to the perfection of charity, already 'consecrated' in the Sacrament of Marriage.

This paragraph is an encouragement of a reality which the community promotes. Here the Holy Father shows his recognition of a type of commitment which couples make within communities such as ours. He is thus indicating two avenues for deepening a theological reflection on this subject.

1. The meaning of consecration. Couples belonging to the community are not ordinary lay people: they pronounce commitments of poverty, chastity and obedience, which means renouncing the autonomy necessary for sanctifying temporal realities in the way of Christians living in the world. From now on, as a family, they are ordained towards another vocation of an eschatological type, in the heart of, and with, the community.

In a certain way they are called to live the demands which are proper to consecrated life in order to be faithful to their calling. However, these demands could never be lived out in the same way as a single person would live them out, because, as John Paul II underlined, the married couple must also assume their duties towards their children.

How can one explain this eschatological vocation specific to couples in the community? If the consecrated celibate members in the community are witnesses to the Kingdom of God, where there is no marriage, the couples and families, in consecrating their conjugal love and their family relationships, in living fully the grace of the sacrament of marriage, already witness to the splendour of human love which allows itself to be penetrated and transfigured by the gift of God, which is divine love. In this way they witness to the call to model all our interpersonal relationships on the relationships of the divine persons. Seeking to live a renunciation of self and the disinterested gift of oneself to the other, the families place themselves at the service of life, conscious of being called to both a human and a supernatural fruitfulness which they must deploy in seeking to listen to God's will together, each one aspiring to an authentic mystical life. In fact, there is an aspect of nuptial love in the mystery of Christ which only married couples can make known.

The Holy Family of Nazareth is an icon, the model and, in a certain sense, the source, of what all Christian families are called to live. This is more especially true of every family in the community because they witness to what family relationships are, and to conjugal love transfigured in the Kingdom of Heaven. The key to this transfiguration here on earth is an

attitude of oblation because 'applied to all our human relationships it transforms them, transfigures them and becomes
a source of fruitfulness'.[3]

2. Charity. The second path leading to a deeper understanding is that of the ultimate aim of consecration: charity.

If the perfection of Mary and Joseph's mutual love is the
icon of conjugal love lived out on earth, the community's families are not alone in being a witness; it is the community
as a whole which witnesses to this love through the desire
manifested by its couples to live this transfiguration of their
conjugal love. In the Kingdom, this transfiguration is a consequence of the gift of the beatific vision: even now on this
earth we can contemplate God through the eyes of faith. It's
normal that couples who desire their conjugal love to be
transfigured should feel a call to a contemplative vocation
(which means to see God through the eyes of faith) and thus
order their whole life to this. So as to respond to this vocation
which presupposes a radical stripping of self, couples use the
same means as Jesus proposes in the Gospel: poverty, obedience, chastity. They will live this however, by respecting the
growth of the community which is a fundamental priority, this
same community being their family.

The value of the ecclesial dimension of Christian marriage
If families are consecrated within the community, it is because
their Christian marriage is already a consecration. Regarding
this, I would like to quote Cardinal Ouellet. In his address to
the bishops of France, he stressed that the Catechism of the
Catholic Church affirms that 'The entire Christian life bears
the mark of the spousal love of Christ and the Church. Already
Baptism, the entry into the People of God, is a nuptial mystery;
it is, so to speak, the nuptial bath (Eph. 5.26–27) which pre-
cedes the wedding feast, the Eucharist.'[4] The sacraments in
general, and marriage in particular, are in fact acts by which
the Bridegroom and the Bride are joined and united, and in
which the divine Bridegroom calls the Church, who is his
Bride, into being. Through the paschal and eucharistic gift of

his body, he engenders, nourishes and purifies her, making her holy and calling her to follow him in his mission (cf. Eph. 5.21–33).

This ecclesial and nuptial perspective of the sacramental is rooted in a rediscovery of the Pauline 'mystery' which, together with the Johannine symbolism of the eucharist and the wedding feast, is the foundation of the New Testament sacramentality. It articulates all the sacraments according to the nuptial mystery of Christ and the Church, whilst being careful to mark the difference between the primordial action of Christ–Spouse and that of the Church–Spouse, which is recipient and subordinate. Thanks to this new perspective, the sacrament of marriage finds itself at the heart of the sacramentality of the Church, closely linked to the eucharist, the greatest covenant mystery. The sacramentality of the Church is expressed in a special way by the sacrament of the couple who become 'one body', sacramentally speaking, in the measure in which the couple is rooted in and nourished by the 'unique body' which is the eucharistic body of Christ and the Church, source and summit of all sacramentality. This is why the 'community of life and love' which a couple and a family form, is rightly referred to as a domestic church because it incarnates the nuptial relationship between Christ and the Church. It is not only an image of this, but a concrete realization founded on the truth of the sacrament of marriage.

This ecclesial dimension of marriage is already apparent in the way in which one distinguishes the effects of the sacrament. *Familiaris Consortio (FC)* underlines that 'the first and immediate effect (*res et sacramentum*) is not the supernatural grace in itself, but the Christian conjugal bond, a communion of two which is typically Christian because it represents the mystery of Christ's incarnation and its covenant mystery'. This Christian conjugal bond, which joins a husband and wife to one another indissolubly, is not first and foremost of a juridical nature: it is a gift of the Holy Spirit which Christ gives when he comes to meet the spouses to bless them, sanctify them and to accept their mutual gift within his own gift to the Church. The first effect of the sacrament is therefore above all ecclesial. It constitutes the couple as a public sign of their belonging radically to the Church by the fact of their mutual gift in the Lord being accepted and blessed, enriched and transformed by God in order to be put at the disposition of the Church. Héribert Mühlen and Louis Ligier speak about this objective ecclesial bond as a 'charism of consecration', which is a source of the supernatural grace given to the couple but not identical to the supernatural grace. One can lose the grace of conjugal union through the fault of the couple's disposition but the ecclesial bond remains indissoluble. It expresses the fact of the couple's belonging to the nuptial mystery of Christ and its objective participation in the sacramentality of the Church.

According to how docile the spouses are in welcoming the Holy Spirit as their bond of love, given to them during the course of the sacramental celebration, they are affirmed humanly speaking in their faithfulness, and consecrated supernaturally for the service of life and spiritual fruitfulness. In this way they become active in the mission of the Church as a couple and as a family. This ecclesial and missionary dimension wasn't at all evident in the past – and still isn't today – because marriage was understood almost exclusively from the point of view of 'nature', even if one affirmed that this was 'raised up' by Christ to the dignity of a sacrament. And this is where the tendency comes from to emphasize only the work of procreation and the children's education. Thus the personal and ecclesial dimension has remained marginal and extrinsic.

In the light of the Second Vatican Council's Christo-centricity, the strictly sacramental, and therefore ecclesial dimension, comes forth from the meeting with Christ which, through the grace of marriage, makes specific the graces of baptism and confirmation, assumes and enriches the couple and their love for its proper ends. In this Christocentric per-spective, the couple is not only blessed and sanctified on a level of 'natural' love, even if this dimension must be carefully inte-grated; the couple is blessed, consecrated and placed at the service of the love of Christ for the Church. 'The Spirit given by the Lord gives them a new heart and renders them – man and woman – capable of loving one another, as Christ has loved us. Conjugal love reaches this fullness to which it is interiorly ordained, that is to say, conjugal charity.'[5] The Christian couple, through their personal offering and their welcome of the sacrament, place themselves at the Lord's disposition in order to express in the 'language of the body' their own nuptial love for the Church. The family, a community 'which is saved' becomes a community 'which saves'.[6] 'Christ our Lord has abundantly blessed this love, which is rich in its various features, coming as it does from the spring of divine life and modelled on Christ's own union with the Church.'[7] Through sacramental marriage, the husband and wife constitute a 'micro-Church' endowed with the properties of the Church: one, holy, Catholic and apostolic. Here we have, in fact, the community of life: priesthood, charity, evangelization and worship. These constituent dimensions confer upon the couple the grace of being an ecclesial reality which is essentially missionary in nature, following the example of the greater Church of which they are a foundational element.

Conclusion

The Lord inspired the hearts of the different Popes of the last century to encourage a fervent prayer to the Holy Spirit among the faithful so that the Spirit would renew the Church and the face she presents to the world. Because, as John Paul II often reminded us, its mission has only just begun. The world has witnessed more changes since the Second Vatican Council than during the preceding 100 years. If the Church needs to adapt herself to a world which is in deep mutation and in danger of losing the meaning of what man is as a result of having denied God, she can only do this by becoming more fully herself. The family seems to be the institution which is most in question.

Also, is it not surprising that the Holy Spirit is at work revealing the depth of the mystery of Christian marriage and raising up the call among certain married couples to live a form of consecration? In this way they become a sign for the Church of what consecrated love between Christian spouses means through the sacrament of marriage. There was a poet who liked to talk about woman being man's future. Consecrated families remind us that communion is the future of humanity itself.

Notes

1. The L'Arche community of Lanza del Vasto, which influenced us at the beginning, had a utopian project: to be an alternative non-violent microsociety. In choosing to enter the Catholic Church, the first members of the community progressively took a distance from this model.
2. John Paul II, *Vita Consecrata*, 62.
3. Ephraïm, 'Maria' (Community of the Beatitudes) July–August 1998, p. 11.
4. Mgr Ouellet, Secretary of the Pontifical Council for the Promotion of Christian Unity, a talk about the sacrament of marriage to the bishops of France gathered for the annual Plenary Assembly at Lourdes, 5 November 2001 (2001, 2259, pp. 1030–50).
5. *FC*, 13.
6. *FC*, 49.
7. *GS*, 48.

4

The Life of the Church: The Sacramental Method of Evangelization

Javier Prades López

Introduction[1]

'Many modern Europeans believe they know what Christianity actually is, but in reality they know not . . . Many baptized persons live as if Christ did not exist . . . For many, a vague and uncommitted religiosity has usurped the great certainties of faith . . . But when the Son of Man comes, will he find faith on earth? (Lk. 18.8). Will He find it in these lands of our Europe, of ancient Christian tradition? It is an open question that indicates with lucidity the profundity and the dramatic nature of the greatest and most serious challenge that our Churches will have to face.'[2]

We shall take this question, posed by John Paul II to all European Christians, as our point of departure. We are moved to do so by the belief that without real knowledge of Christianity, the concrete life of every man and woman loses all prospect of attaining to complete happiness during his or her sojourn on earth. For of course, one can have constant recourse to the vocabulary of Christianity, while living as though Christ did not exist, but that hardly constitutes 'real knowledge' of him. And so pressing is the desire for happiness in every human being that we cannot cease to ask ourselves why it is that Europeans in our time do not know Christ. At the same time, we can only wonder about the consequences of such ignorance.[3]

Let us not equivocate about our point of departure. It would, for example, be a mistake to suppose that the crisis we are facing could be adequately addressed by anything so superficial as the use of more effective means to communicate the faith, or the implementation of certain changes in ecclesial structures, or the adoption of certain values seemingly more appealing to the present era. In truth, we would be gravely mistaken if our diagnosis of Europe's spiritual crisis and any response we might make to that crisis did not speak directly to the ultimate level of human existence, where the question of life's meaning is in play. Only at this level do the criteria of the faith really matter, because only at this level can they so affect us that our lives can change.

John Paul II himself pointed out, in effect, some of the symptoms of a humanity that would do without the Gospel in day-to-day life. The Pope alluded to a darkening of hope, at the root of which is an anthropology without Christ, from which derives a fear of the future, the fragmentation of existence, a growing degradation in interpersonal relations. All these are indicative of the widespread growth of a certain nihilism among us, variously at work in the pragmatism and cultural relativism so prevalent in our day. One is led to the worrisome conclusion that our society can be characterized as a 'culture of death'.[4]

Since we ourselves are Europeans, we cannot deceive ourselves into thinking that the symptoms identified by the Holy Father only affect others, and concern us only in the measure that we would assist them in their plight. His observations have to do first of all with us. It is our own existence that is imperilled. It is our freedom and our reason that are at stake in a vertiginous drama: whether to accept or to reject the real presence of Christ in all the particulars of our daily lives.

The following remarks are inspired by my reading of one of the primary texts of the late Mgr Luigi Giussani, *Why the Church?*[5] My intention is to highlight the nature of the Christian fact and its methodological implications. In this way, I hope to offer an initial approach to the thought of a fellow European whose lifework constitutes one of the greatest contributions in the last half-century to the rediscovery of the abiding novelty of Christ. His experience as a teacher, in the truest and deepest sense of that word, has been at once an expression and a font of rigorous reflection, the style and substance of which has aptly been described as 'generative thought', that is to say, thought that is itself born of experience and is in turn richly capable of generating an experience.[6] My objective is not so much to introduce you to his work, still less to summarize it. What I propose to do on this occasion is much simpler: to engage in an act of personal reflection as illumined by his thought. I undertake such a reflection in the hope that it might serve as an invitation to you to read him yourself.

Any adequate reflection on the Church and contemporary man, requires, in my judgement, the effort of a 'double focus'. On the one hand, one must have a 'sacramental focus': a profound appreciation of the Church's sacramental nature, which is derived from the redemptive incarnation. On the other hand, an 'anthropological focus' is also required: in other words, a profound appreciation of the human being as a creature, finite and sinful, with respect to the sacramental nature of the Church.[7] So it is necessary to ask oneself about the difficulties posed by contemporary opinion to this double focus.

I shall proceed as follows: after a closer look at the cultural diagnosis offered by John Paul II, I will describe the Church's original nature as an event. I shall then propose that the Church's sacramental method is derived from revelation. Next I shall describe the condition proper to man regarding his adherence to the 'sign' that is the Church. To conclude, I shall offer a few final observations about the sort of education that is necessary for the mission of lay people in today's world.

The malaise of our time: an eviscerated faith

The confusion between Christian faith and vague religiosity
John Paul II affirmed that many of our contemporaries do not really know what Christianity is; they do not understand it, and so confuse it with a vague religiosity. We should discuss this phenomenon in further detail, because it can be rather difficult to understand at first sight. The Pope was not referring here to an opposition to Christianity that proceeds more or less violently from without (although this also occurs). More precisely, he sought to identify a subtle process of evacuation

from within of the faith, and its progressive confusion with mere religiosity. This degradation can be more easily seen when it produces the sort of syncretism that is all too common nowadays, wherein we find a great variety of elements foreign to the faith, such as Eastern meditational techniques, pagan spirituality of a New Age stripe, or cocktails involving features of a variety of other religions or political ideologies, Buddhism, the Kabbalah, environmentalism, anti-globalism – to name but a few. To consider in any detail the challenges posed by these currents of modern religiosity, and the influence they are having on many Christians today, is something that deserves an entire conference. What interests us on the present occasion is to identify this progressive weakening of the Christian faith from within, and its consequences for believers.

Our problem, then, does not so much concern a more or less accurate analysis of the particular array of external influences currently at work. The proof is that already in the middle of the nineteenth century, Newman had pointed out that

> religion, as being personal, should be real; but, except within a small range of subjects, it commonly is not real in England ... Objects are barely necessary to it ... Its doctrines are not so much facts as stereotyped aspects of facts; and it is afraid, so to say, of walking round them ... I am not denying that the assent which it inculcates and elicits is genuine as regards its contracted range of doctrine, but it is at best notional.[8]

It is in our interests to take Newman's claim seriously, and to ask ourselves how Christianity could really elicit genuine assent, such that we might rise above the situation described by John Paul II: namely, that Europeans do not really know what Christianity is. In effect, for many people today, Christianity is more notional than real, and this is the case not only as regards those who have already abandoned the faith, but unfortunately also for many who participate, more or less intensely, in the Christian community. It is necessary to go deeper into this phenomenon, without becoming distracted by other problems, important though they are, because they do not go to the root of the malaise we detect in so many Christians in our society.

The five 'withouts' of modern rationalism

Mgr Giussani sought to address this issue since the 1950s, when, in Catholic Italy, he first noticed that although young people declared themselves Christians, their allegiance was only nominal, since it did not have any direct bearing on their lives.[9] Since then, he consistently affirmed that this malaise stems from the collapse of faith as the effectual recognition that Christ is all in all.[10] He described the existential evacuation or evisceration of faith by invoking five harmful characteristics, which he calls the 'five "withouts" of modern rationalism'.[11]

The key to his diagnosis is that if the exceptional presence of Christ, which fully responds to the demands of human reason, is not historically acknowledged, this presence will be confused with something less than it; this results, in turn, in the erection of idols, more or less religious in form, and though these idols may be based upon something real, they falsely ascribe to some feature that is proper to the mystery alone. Let us examine a synthesis of these symptoms as they can be seen in daily experience.

If we deny that Christ, in his Body that is the Church, offers us the only complete access to the mystery of God, we strip him of his personal and ecclesial concreteness. In this way, we eliminate the possibility of a human experience of the mystery, because we spurn spatial-temporal reality as the place where we can discover the ultimate meaning of life. What, then, is left? In the best of cases, Christian terminology remains, although it has lost its real meaning. The existential consequence is that we give in to the idolatry of whatever aspect of reality lies before us, because we take one of life's factors – work, affective relationships, one's culture or ethnicity – as what is truly divine in life, which is to say, as that which ultimately defines existence. We have, then, a god without a face: a god that conforms itself to whatever images or projects we have manufactured for ourselves, and thus is unable to challenge our human position. Such a god makes us slaves, in each passing moment, to evanescent appearances.

If the Church is not lived as the site of Christ's presence, then it does not embrace all the personal and social dimensions of human existence, and runs the risk, accordingly, of seeing itself reduced to either clericalism or spiritualism. Clericalism turns its back on reality and fosters an ecclesial self-absorption; correlatively, it inevitably conceives of the Church in terms of power. As Augustine reminds us, however, the Church is nothing other than the world reconciled with God, *Reconciliatus mundus, Ecclesia*: the world is renewed if the mystery of Christ enters actively into all of its facets and transforms them. Dualistic spirituality also separates faith from life: its faith is merely juxtaposed with life instead of being the graceful illumination of human reason and renewal of human affection in day-to-day existence. Spiritualism and clericalism both continue to use the vocabulary of Christianity, but it is used in a sentimentally reductionistic fashion, which is to say that it is devoid of any real significance. And in both cases, the Church effectively ceases to be an active protagonist in history. In the words of Péguy, cited by Giussani: 'Since they don't have the courage to be in the world, they believe they are with God. Since they don't have the courage to be on the side of men, they believe they are on God's side. Since they don't love anyone, they believe they love God.'

When the Church loses the world, the world becomes depersonalized and alienated. The human 'I' is no longer in a condition that allows it to mature as a person, and it is left at the mercy of circumstances emptied of meaning. What is at stake is human freedom, which, even if it is not threatened by the edicts of totalitarianism, is at risk in contemporary social practice, where we do even more to cultivate a 'culture of death'. The great categories of human existence – life, work, affection, time and space – are interpreted in an inhuman way. Chesterton astutely explains how the determinism characteristic of agnosticism pushed him toward the Church, not so much in the name of the 'other world' but from an understanding of 'this world' that respected common sense, and above all from his experience of himself as free and therefore also responsible.[12] The genuine mark of Christ's victory in the world is visible precisely due to the fact that from within the concrete circumstances of life, it calls forth a free 'I', a person able to live freely within those same circumstances. Contrarily, an alienated 'I' is an 'I' without God: an 'I' that cannot escape the tedium and nausea so characteristic of our contemporary malaise; an 'I' that abandons itself to chance and oscillates between moments of irrational exaltation and existential despair. This is how one 'abandons oneself to the void' (C. Fabro) in an age in which a soft nihilism prevails: a nihilism more conformist than revolutionary, within a society that has turned transgression into something ordinary.

The Church as the event of salvation

The salvific dialogue of Christ with each person
Through his life, death and resurrection, Jesus Christ has revealed the mystery of the Father. This is how truth is made manifest in the life of mankind. Each one of us reaches the truth about his life when his own story is incorporated into the singular story of Jesus of Nazareth, who, by the Spirit of the Resurrected One, lives in the Church. Jesus is, thus, the path by which human beings in all ages and places come to the Father. The salvific dialogue between the Father and the historically situated person is through the mediation of his son Jesus Christ and the Holy Spirit, realized in the person's encounter with the Church.[13]

In making that claim, we exclude from the outset any conception of the Church that would reduce it to a mere association, a merely human aggregate orientated toward the satisfaction of the religious, spiritual or moral needs of its members.[14] On the contrary, we are dealing with the perfectly free encounter of the human being with the Triune God, according to the modality in which God has sought to manifest himself in history. It is extremely important to perceive straightaway what is distinctive about this approach, because its consequences are (as we shall see later) decisive. In the former conception, the Church is what it is thanks to man, for whom the Church is an expression of his most noble feelings, lived in community with other men in accordance with some project that he has set for himself; his membership in the Church consequently takes on a voluntary character, analogous to participation in an altruistic association.[15] In the latter case, however, we are dealing with an exceptional encounter, unforeseeable the moment before it occurs, which awakens in us the recognition of an extraordinary affinity with the deepest needs of the human heart. We do not have to do here simply with the fulfilment of an individual's personal project but with the surprise of an unexpected encounter, fully correspondent with the needs of the heart, which is therefore embraced in wonder and with gratitude. It is enough to turn to the pages of the Gospel to realize that James's and Andrew's, or Matthew's encounter with Jesus was not the result of some plan they had formulated, but rather the wondrous and profoundly grateful recognition of a reality that had irrupted into their lives. Neither Matthew nor Nathaniel were expecting Jesus when he approached them; and when John and Andrew went to see the man they had been told about, he completely exceeded their expectations and anticipations.[16] Hence, Giussani affirms that 'The unity of Christianity is not a thought nor an ideology; not even the learning of a doctrine. It's not an idea or a philosophy, but the proposal of a Presence: the Incarnation is a Fact'.[17] The encounter with this presence is, by its very nature, historical and totalizing. In other words, from the very first instant, it demonstrates that it has a claim to make on all aspects of human life, internal and external, past, present and future. It purports to be life's very salvation.[18]

The Christian notion of mystery

At this juncture, and to anticipate somewhat, we would do well briefly to note that when using the word 'mystery', in accordance with the tradition of the (Pauline) New Testament and the liturgy, we do not seek merely to point (however haltingly) to the unknown, and therefore to the unattainable character, whether dark or fearsome, of the divine. Given his incomprehensible infinitude and our finite capacity, we cannot logically rule out the possibility that the mystery can be difficult to grasp.[19] What is typical of the Christian conception of mystery, however, is that, while not denying God's incomprehensibility, it holds that the mystery reveals himself to our finite capacity and enters into the ambit of our experience. In a Christian sense, the mystery is mysterious in so far as when it gives itself to be known experientially.[20]

Within time and space: a historical fact
The form in and by which the mystery has given itself to be known experientially is that of a historical fact. As Newman observed:

> Christianity has been long enough in the world to justify us in dealing with it as a fact in the world's history ... It may indeed legitimately be made the subject-matter of theories ... but to a fact do they relate, on an admitted fact do they turn, which must be ascertained as other facts ... Christianity is no theory of the study or the cloister ... It has from the first had an objective existence.[21]

With these words the great English thinker highlights the very nature of the Christian event, which is, in the first place, a unique fact, occurring in the time and space of human history: the incarnation, life, passion, death and resurrection of Jesus of Nazareth, the son of the Father.

Of course, from this fact stems all of the doctrinal, moral and spiritual consequences that constitute the great wealth of the Catholic tradition. Every attempt to disconnect the fact from its significance or meaning has always been doomed to failure, because only the intrinsic unity of the fact and its meaning does justice to the method by which God has chosen to reveal himself.[22] But the doctrinal and moral elements of the tradition can only maintain their importance in the measure that they corroborate the original fact. In our era, in which it is so easy to accept a Christianity reduced to morality or

spirituality, and thereby emptied of any effectual relationship
to the incarnation and its method, it would be wise to pay heed
to the words of T. S. Eliot:

> Then came, at a predetermined moment, a moment in time
> and of time,
> A moment not out of time, but in time, in what we call his-
> tory: transecting, bisecting the world of time, a moment in
> time but not like a moment of time,
> A moment in time but time was made through that moment:
> for without the meaning there is no time, and that moment
> of time gave the meaning.[23]

Christianity is exactly this irruption of the mystery of God
in a specific moment in history, which purports to provide a
definitive answer to the question as to why history exists.

To the comprehensiveness of the Christian fact, at once historical and absolute, modern rationalism has opposed itself by
seeking to tame or limit it. At least since Kant's reduction of
Christianity to 'the limits of pure reason', if not before, it has
generally been deemed to be simply impossible that an historical fact, given in time and space, could bear within it the
absolute significance of the mystery for the salvation of men.
The life of Jesus is taken to be merely historical, a temporal
occurrence like any other; and because such facts progressively succumb to the oblivion of the past, the most we can
hope, according to the view now dominant, is to preserve
something of the doctrinal and moral consequences of his
life.[24] On the basis of this radical domestication of the Christian fact, various ethical or spiritual reductionisms of Christianity have emerged. Perhaps they meant well, and intended
only to assure Christianity's continuance in modern societies;
but however that may be, the result has been the complete
reinterpretation of its original nature.[25] We have already dis-
cussed how the logic of modern rationalism plays out existentially, in the present situation, in the evisceration of Christian
faith.

The perpetual presence of the fact in history:
the contemporaneity of Christ with every man

John Paul II affirmed that the Church guarantees the 'contemporaneity of Christ' to every man.[26] This felicitous expression shows that the genius of Catholicism, which is capable of overcoming the objections of modern rationalism, is to ensure the permanence of the Christian fact in history, so that human beings in every age and place may enter into the dialogue of salvation with God. We are clearly reminded of this by John Paul II's apostolic exhortation on Europe:

> Jesus is present, alive and acting through the Church: He is in the Church and the Church is in Him (cf. Jn 15.1ff.; Gal. 3.28; Eph. 4.15–16; Acts 9.5). In the Church, through the gift of the Holy Spirit, continues without ceasing His work of Salvation. With the eyes of faith we can see the mysterious signs of Christ in the diverse signs that He has given us.[27]

In effect, if the Church were not a concrete human reality, visibly proximate in its signs, it could not appeal to my freedom and urge it to its realization. Were the Church not as the Pope described it, not only would our relation to Christ cease to be contemporary to him, it would be merely a sentimental or pious memory subject, in the final analysis, to my arbitrariness, incapable of changing me beyond my own measure.

We are considering the Church and its nature strictly because we are interested in knowing and loving Jesus, and in him, the Father in heaven.[28] It is of the utmost importance that we recuperate a conception of the Church that situates ecclesiology within a Christological and trinitarian horizon. In the light of the mystery of the incarnation, we should also be able to perceive the mystery of the Church in terms of the 'method' by which eternal life is conveyed to us; and eternal life is 'that they should know you, the only true God, and the one whom you sent, Jesus Christ' (Jn 17.1–2). Hence Giussani affirms that 'the crucial problem of the Church as the continuity of Christ cannot be grasped unless it is seen as analogous to the problem of Christ himself. The Church is the method

Christ uses for self-communication in time and space, just as Christ is the method God felt he should use to communicate himself to men and so establish their means of salvation.'[29]

The reactions that the mystery of the Church elicits will, of necessity, be analogous to those elicited by the mystery of Jesus: fascination in some, violent rejection in others.[30] Newman knew enough to see that the contemporaneity of Christ was not interrupted with his ascension to heaven, such that we might also know the wonders of his grace and his indestructible power:

> If they were blessed who lived in primitive times, and saw the fresh traces of their Lord, and heard the echoes of Apostolic voices, blessed too are we whose special portion it is to see that same Lord revealed in His Saints. The wonders of His grace in the soul of man, its creative power, its inexhaustible resources, its manifold operation, all this we know, as they knew it not.[31]

Thanks to this singular prolonging of the Christian event, it is possible for us to have exactly the same astonishing and gracious encounter with his Presence, so that it is possible once again to travel on the path of faith as the path that realizes our freedom to the fullest, situated historically in the here and now. This is why the Church interests us: in the measure that it makes possible a living relationship with Christ. As Kierkegaard so astutely observed, the only sort of relationship that allows one to judge life in a decisive way is a relationship with a living person, not a dead one.

If it is difficult to perceive existentially the importance of this singular method, chosen by God, by which he is present in the signs of his Church (in its sacramental life and in the lives of its saints), perhaps we will let ourselves be touched by Charles Péguy's profession of amazement, expressed at once with great emotion and great restraint, at the method by which God has remained in history:

> Miracle of miracles, my child, mystery of mysteries.
> Because Jesus Christ has become our carnal brother

Because he has pronounced, carnally and in time, eternal
words [. . .]
It is to us, the weak, that was given,
He depends on us, weak and carnal,
To bring to life and to nourish and to keep alive in time
These words pronounced alive in time.
Mystery of mysteries, this privilege that was given to us,
This incredible, exorbitant privilege,
To keep alive the words of life,
To nourish with our blood, with our flesh, with our heart
The words which, without us, would collapse fleshless [. . .]
It belongs to us, it depends on us to assure the words
An eternal perpetuity, a carnal perpetuity,
A perpetuity nourished with meat, with fat and with
blood.[32]

The sacramental method of revelation: incarnation and Church

Both Eliot and Péguy show the reciprocal relationship
between historical temporality and divine eternity, between
the visibility of the flesh and the invisibility of the mystery, a
relationship given in unity 'without confusion or division'[33] in
the mystery of Christ and in the Church. Thanks to this surprising structure of the incarnation and of the Church, it is
possible to recognize the actual permanence of Christ and his
saving initiative with respect to the historically situated freedom of every man. What Péguy and Eliot have intuited is at
the very heart of a Catholic understanding of the Church, and
it marks the original difference between the Christian fact
and any other religious or philosophical vision. This is not to
deny that much that is worthy in philosophical and religious
experience has been integrated and brought to fulfilment in
the Catholic tradition. So it is that we have come to the core of
what we earlier referred to as the 'sacramental focus' requisite
for a proper understanding of the Church.

An orthodox Catholic vision

According to Mgr Giussani, the only possible position that can fully respect the sacramental character of revelation and, therefore, also of the Church, is what he calls 'the orthodox Catholic vision', inasmuch as it is the continuous embodiment of the Christian tradition: 'the main characteristic of the orthodox Catholic attitude is that it is consistent with the structure of the Christian event as it presented itself in history'.[34] This is the case thanks to the Church's 'method' – the 'encounter', which is to say, the apparently fortuitous meeting with a personal reality external to oneself, an objective presence that, although irreducibly 'other' to oneself, moves one's heart nevertheless. That the word 'encounter' is particularly suitable here has to do with the fact that it 'has an exterior connotation just as decisive as the interior one'.[35] The reality that the Church embodies is not 'merely' spiritual, but incarnate, even material, as tangible as any other thing that exists in our common world.

This orthodox Catholic vision has the capacity to supersede and so also integrate two other common positions, neither of which affords adequate access to the problem of the Church: one that would reduce Christianity to just another fact in the past (the rationalistic attitude), and a second that tends to limit the reality borne by the Church to an interior illumination (the Protestant attitude).[36] The Catholic position supersedes these two positions because it maintains the mysterious coincidence that exists between the presence of Jesus and the visible reality of his disciples, manifest while he was still on earth, when he sent them from village to village, two by two, having told them that 'Anyone who listens to you listens to me.'[37] Jesus teaches his disciples in a variety of ways that they participate in his very life and produce the same effects that he does, indeed even greater ones,[38] in the measure they are assimilated into his personal reality: thus, for example, his images of the vine and the branches,[39] and of the one body.[40] These show that the divine reality itself is communicated to the disciples through the unity that exists between them and with Jesus. As the apostle John writes: 'life was made visible:

we saw it and we are giving our testimony . . . What we have seen and heard we are telling you so that you may be in union with us.'[41]

The fullness of this sacramental logic, characteristic of the orthodox Catholic vision, reaches its climax at the Last Supper, on Holy Thursday, when Jesus, anticipating his very offering of himself to the Father on the cross, institutes the sacraments of holy orders and the eucharist, in order to guarantee the permanence of his memory in the sacramental gesture, 'Do this in memory of me.'[42] In this gesture, the personal action of Jesus and his binding himself to the objective moment of the rite (eucharist-ministry) coincide in such a way that the gesture is converted into a paradigmatic moment, from which is drawn the simultaneously objective and personal nature of the Church.[43] The disciples see themselves efficaciously interpellated in their freedom by the personal activity of Jesus, who is present among them, and by means of this gesture, are incorporated into the sacramental sign that perpetuates his personal presence. By means of the disciples, then, the diffusion of Christ's witness to all human beings over the course of history is, through the power of the Holy Spirit, made possible.[44]

The 'logic of the sign' in the incarnation and in the Church: the invisible in and through the visible

1. The *Catechism of the Catholic Church* affirms that everything in the life of Jesus is a sign of his Mystery. By his gestures, his miracles and his words, he has revealed that 'in him dwells the whole fullness of the deity bodily' (Col. 2.9). His humanity appears therefore as the 'sacrament', in other words, the sign and instrument of his divinity and of the salvation that he brings with him: what was visible in his earthly life leads to the invisible mystery of his divine affiliation and his redemptive mission.[45]

The same 'sacramental logic' is reflected in the liturgy of Christmas: 'thanks to the mystery of the Word made flesh, the light of your glory shown before our eyes so that, knowing God visibly, he will lead us to the love of the invisible'.[46] And, with

St Irenaeus, the Church's *lex orandi* finds the witness of the Greek patristic tradition: 'For man does not see God by his own powers; but if He pleases, He is seen by men, by those whom He wills, and when He wills, and as He wills.'[47] The Eastern patristic tradition also reflects this same awareness, as is witnessed by St Ephraem, in his hymns *De fide* and *De nativitate*,[48] as does the Latin tradition, with St Augustine at its head:

> Life itself has manifested itself in the flesh, so that by this manifestation, that which could only be seen by the heart could be seen also with the eyes, and in this form heal hearts. Because the Word can only be seen with the heart, but the flesh is also seen with bodily eyes. We were able to see the flesh, but we were not able to see the Word. *The Word became flesh*, which we can see, to heal in us that which makes us unable to see the Word.[49]

St Thomas Aquinas continues this tradition in the Middle Ages.[50]

Giussani frequently repeats that when the mystery reveals himself, he reveals himself as mystery. In other words, he maintains a unity between his communication to man and to his insurmountable transcendence.[51] God has drawn so near that he has communicated himself visibly in the Son, and at the same time he preserves his invisibility. Irenaeus put it beautifully:

> And for this reason did the Word become the dispenser of the paternal grace for the benefit of men . . . revealing God indeed to men, but presenting man to God, and preserving at the same time the invisibility of the Father, lest man should at any time become a despiser of God, and that he should always possess something towards which he might advance; but, on the other hand, revealing God to men through many dispensations, lest man, falling away from God altogether, should cease to exist.[52]

When God manifests himself, on the one hand, we are granted an unmistakable familiarity with the mystery of salvation, to the point that one may speak of 'God with us'.[53] On the other hand, he makes us fully aware that he is invisible and that no one has ever seen Him,[54] that he is immortal and incorruptible, and that he is the 'Almighty'.[55] If we can say, with St Augustine, *'Deus intimior intimo meo'* (God is closer to me than I am to myself) by way of emphasizing the surprising union of God with man, the faith of the Church has also always insisted on acknowledging the 'greater dissimilarity' as insurmountable: God is, in other words, equally *superior summo meo*.[56] In this manner, the ineffable transcendence of the mystery of God is respected, and so also preserves us from any idolatrous reductionism.

One of the finer contributions to theology by the Swiss theologian Hans Urs von Balthasar lies in his appeal to aesthetic experience in order to think about Christian revelation. Thus, in aesthetic intuition, beauty is in the first instance a visible 'form' whose light does not issue from some source other than the form, but emerges rather from its own depths. The visibility and the inwardness of the aesthetic form are inseparable, because the content is not behind the form, as though the form were merely a pretext, but within it.[57] So too, the person who does not stand in wonder before the form will never have access to its contents.[58] By analogy, in the event of Christ it is the 'form' that is revealed in a content that is not off somewhere else but rather within its own depth. Jesus reveals, and at the same time conceals or preserves, the ultimate mystery of his origin in the Father, and the difference between the sign and the mystery that he is cannot be overcome, because it is not available to man: 'whoever has seen me has seen the Father',[59] and there is no way to approach God the Father that would avoid or otherwise attempt to get around Jesus. The historical figure of Jesus, who acts by the power of the Holy Spirit, is received as the appearance of a divine depth that surpasses all worldly nature.[60]

2. We have seen that in the sacrament of the Church and the gift of the Spirit the mystery of Christ is contemporaneous with the present moment in history.[61] What is at issue here is the very continuance of Jesus himself, in a manner that is

incomparably more real than any human institution could possibly attribute to its founder.[62] That is why it is not quite correct to say that the Church is but *a* or even *the* means of salvation. More precisely, the Church is salvation in its historical and visible form.[63] De Lubac affirmed that the mission of the Church was to re-present Christ, in the strong sense in which this expression was used in Christian antiquity, which is to say that it makes him present.[64] De Lubac also maintained that the Church had never abandoned this mission, without which its activity would lack an objective, and, what is worse, the world would lose its redemption.[65] The Church's mission, so decisive for the destiny of the world, is possible due to its sacramental nature.

Only in the unity of the visible sign and the invisible mystery can the possibility of repeating the very same experience that the disciples had when they were with Jesus be perpetuated. The encyclical *Fides et Ratio* has used the expression 'sacramental character' to designate the originality that is proper to Christian revelation, through the visible signs that make freedom possible (53). The encyclical thereby advances the profound intuitions of Vatican II, which, when speaking of the nature of revelation, identifies it as the manifestation of the 'sacramental mystery of his will' (*'notum facere sacramentum voluntatis suae . . .'*) by means of deeds and words (*'haec revelationis oeconomia fit gestis verbisque intrinsece inter se connexis'*).[66] The divine economy has the character of *sacramentum* that is revealed by way of the intrinsic unity of words and deeds in the person of Jesus and in the apostolic transmission of the faith.

The next step in an analysis of the Church's sacramental nature ought to explain how its elements – word, sacrament and the charisms of the Spirit – are, as institutional and charismatic dimensions that proceed from the Holy Spirit, coessential for the correct understanding of the constitution of the Church. But such a discussion exceeds the bounds of this essay.[67]

Let us proceed, then, to consider the relationship between the sacramental sign and the human being, understood as a spiritual being, endowed with reason and freedom, and incarnated in time and space. It is this that we have called the 'anthropological focus' of ecclesiology.

Man's historical condition: reality as sign of the truth, and our openness to that sign

If what has been said thus far is correct, we can understand why the Church does not constitute a substitute for human freedom but rather allows for its realization.

It is very common today to reproach the Church for imposing its point of view, doctrinal or moral, upon the faithful, with the alleged result that human desires are frustrated or suppressed. For certain sectors of public opinion, statements made by the Church that concern doctrine – for example, the uniqueness and universality of Christ, or the refusal to ordain women – or human morality – regarding cloning, contraception or divorce, for example – simply cannot be accepted, because they are thought to threaten human freedom. That is why it is of the utmost importance to demonstrate what human freedom is and how the sacramental nature of the Church, far from suffocating our freedom, in truth makes it possible.[68]

If doctrinal and moral statements do not find their foundation in the living event of Christ, then there remains only a Christianity reduced to morality and spirituality: a Christianity that might, for a time, be socially accepted but that in the long run would continue to exist only at the price of progressively eliminating anything that proved contrary to the spirit of the times. The resistance of our contemporaries to accept the doctrinal and moral teachings of the Church clearly shows the diagnostic prowess of John Paul II: a great many Europeans simply do not know what Christianity truly is. They judge it only by its consequences, and these seem unbearable to them, since their freedom has not encountered the efficacious sign of Christ's real presence, namely, the Church. Without forcing the paradox, one could say that contemporary criticism of Christianity has the salutary effect of making it impossible, in fact, to reduce Christianity to a mere ethic or spirituality. Either we are before the event of a living Christ or Christianity is a hopeless case.

It is the sacramental nature of the Church that makes it possible for any of us to have the same experience as those who met Christ some two thousand years ago. The encounter with the personal truth about Jesus not only elicited from each disciple an intellectual assent but also appealed in each of them to the whole of his person, as a creature both rational and free, through the promise of a meaning that would become his own in that free adherence that we call discipleship: 'Come, and you will see.'[69] All who participated in that encounter experienced a profound transformation of their religious and moral conceptions, which would, at times, evoke an incomprehension bordering on scandal.[70] But they could welcome such a change precisely because their personal adherence to Jesus Christ conferred upon them a new principle of knowledge and action, and transformed them into agents or protagonists of a new culture.[71] Let the witness of the Roman rhetorician Marius Victorinus suffice, when upon his conversion he exclaimed: 'When I found Christ I discovered my humanity.'[72] Without this experience of an encounter with the person of Christ, an encounter that corresponds fully to the needs of the human heart but that is also, nevertheless, a matter of pure grace, an unforeseen, unforseeable and unmerited gift, no one of us could truly live a Christian life. Given the present human condition, no one would be able to respond in a stable and enduring way to the doctrinal and moral demands of revelation, no matter how much they express the truth, in a purely conceptual way, about the fullness of what is human.[73]

Let us turn again to Eliot, who articulates with great clarity and force the fact that only the unity of the visible and the invisible in the ecclesial sign is adequate for a man whose spirit is incarnate:

For Man is joined spirit and body,
And therefore must serve as spirit and body.
Visible and invisible, two worlds meet in Man;
Visible and invisible must meet in His Temple;
You must not deny the body.

Now you shall see the Temple completed:
After much striving, after many obstacles; . . .
The visible reminder of Invisible Light . . .
. . . we thank Thee for our little light . . .
We thank Thee who hast moved us to building, to finding, to forming
at the ends of our fingers and beams of our eyes.
And when we have built an altar to the Invisible Light, we may set
thereon the little lights for which our bodily vision is made . . .
O Light Invisible, we give Thee thanks for Thy great glory![74]

Almost in the manner of a commentary on this passage, Giussani maintains that,

man is a composite of perceivable experience and attitudes that come from within, and both these factors must be present if humanity is to be fulfilled to the utmost in the unfolding of a given event. And Christianity, in making its urgent appeal to freedom of conscience, and given its concern for tangible things, responds to both these factors.[75]

Giussani often invoked the phrase 'coincidence between sign and mystery' to express the Christological identity in differentiating of the visible flesh and invisible divinity.[76] Through the mediation of this formulation, he connects the sacramental character of the Church with its anthropological relevance by showing how, in an unexpected but most profound way, the nature of Christian revelation and the very structure of the human being correspond. In effect, the sacramental modality of the mystery's self-manifestation makes it possible really to know our human experience in so a deep way that we arrive at the mystery, and to exert our freedom as an

historic adherence to the real sign of his presence. 'The sacrament really is the divine act of the Risen Christ who
knocks on the door of our personality ... It is this bond with
man's freedom of conscience that precisely distinguishes the
Christian mystery from the pagan mysteries.'[77] Only in this
manner can the dynamisms proper to mankind – the capacity to reason and freedom – be brought to fulfilment in the
spiritual creature by satisfying the human need for
happiness.

Let us briefly consider each of these dynamisms in turn.

1. When man's capacity for reason encounters Christ, he
becomes capable of knowing the mystery as revealed within
the ambit of his own experience.[78] God reveals himself and
makes himself experienced in a human reality by way of the
Church that continues the event of Christ in history.[79] 'For the
Church, mystery indicates what lies beyond our capacity for
knowledge, insofar as the Mystery, by sovereign initiative,
desired to make itself knowable within human experience, in a
permanent, faithful way.'[80]

In the coincidence of sign and mystery, which implies
neither confusion nor separation, it is possible to affirm what
is original to the Christian. One cannot know God in his
intimacy without Christ and the Church because

> what has been revealed to us by the Mystery himself, what
> has been given to us in Revelation, is the man, Jesus Christ.
> This man is the synthesis and the center of all that the
> Mystery has sought to convey to human beings ... There
> exists no knowledge of the Mystery (apart from human
> reductions of it) if it is not through this man, Jesus of Naza-
> reth, through whose nature God chose to reveal himself and
> thereby communicate to man as Mystery. Man and Mys-
> tery, this was Jesus, this is Jesus, this will be Jesus. 'Christ
> yesterday, today and always'.[81]

That is why faith is a distinctive way to exercise our reason
– and by grace, to be sure – attain to the only object that can
truly fulfil us, an object that is not accessible to us by our
own efforts. Faith is a new and gratuitous way to exercise our

reason 'understood as the awareness of reality'.[82] The man of faith exercises his reason as the capacity to form a judgement about the reality he has before him, in accordance with all its factors; in such a judgement, he departs from the domain of what clearly appears to him, not so as to overcome appearances or to abandon them, but in order to recognize them precisely as the appearance of being, and, in the final analysis, as the mystery of God himself.[83] Only when man understands the nexus between life's concrete circumstances and the bountiful initiative of the mystery can he say that his reason has reached its fulfilment. Otherwise, he will remain on the threshold of the indecipherable enigma of the unknown. Thus, the illuminating power of the grace of faith is precisely to allow the Christian to judge his circumstances in a reasonable way, and so discern the connection between them and the mystery of God.[84]

2. We can recognize an analogous dynamism at work with respect to our freedom and its realization. Let us see how Giussani understands this dynamic, especially since it is out of a concern for human freedom that the rejection of the Christian proposal most often occurs nowadays.[85]

The experience of freedom can be described in a very simple manner: it is the experience that we have when a desire is satisfied. That is why, for a human being, freedom's path sets out from the urgings and indications of one's desires. Here we might invoke St Thomas's celebrated *desiderium naturale videndi Deum*, for it is this desire, inscribed in our hearts by God, that specifies the real meaning of our freedom. Moreover, the heart's deepest longing is not altogether 'other-worldly'. For it is awakened in the encounter with everyday reality, the encounter with what attracts us in the here and now. Of course, the realization of human desire will not be satisfied by finite things; but our desire for the infinite is nourished in our lives by such things, which therefore serve as 'signs'. This means in turn, though, that we will experience the joy that is freedom fulfilled in this our present life only if it is possible to find ourselves somehow in the company of an infinite presence, of the mystery, in precisely the same way that we happen to encounter the sorts of things that offer us finite or quotidian satisfaction.

If, therefore, the dynamic of freedom requires that we enter ever more deeply into the reality that lies before us, that we seek out what exists all the way to its mysterious origin, and if this is the only way that our hearts can rest satisfied, then it is decisive that we encounter signs that coincide completely with the mystery. And surely this is just what is signified by Christ's humanity, and by its continuation in and through and by the Church. In short, properly Christian companionship makes possible something unheard of: namely, that a person's relationship with all the things that he lives each day be the circumstances in which the presence of the mystery of God becomes manifest, and so liberate him, make him free. It is this way that describes authentic human religiosity, which Christ does not annihilate but rather perfects, through the gift of the Holy Spirit. How right it is, then, that we aspire to the eternal at every moment!

3. The encounter with Jesus Christ, which occurs historically within the Church, is thus the critical factor for all of human experience because it manifests in a gratuitous fashion the foundation of the relationship between man and the mystery: the mystery that is the culmination of human experience and so makes the completion or actualization of man's freedom possible. It is the sacramental gesture – of divine origin – that allows for the realization of a free human act, the object of which is the totality of one's own life and of the meaning of what exists. C.S. Lewis understood this truth very well, as is evident from his marvellous reflections on the coincidence between the sign – in this case, his wife – and the mystery of Christ, known and loved precisely through the knowledge and love he had for his wife:

> The most precious gift that marriage gave me was this constant impact of something very close and intimate yet all the time unmistakably other, resistant – in a word, real . . . I need Christ, not something that resembles Him. I want H., not something that is like her . . . My idea of God is not a

divine idea. It has to be shattered time after time. He shatters it Himself. Could we not almost say that this shattering is one of the marks of His presence? The Incarnation is the supreme example; it leaves all previous ideas of the Messiah in ruins . . . In that respect loving her has become, in its measure, like loving Him . . . Not my idea of God but God. Not my idea of H., but H.[86]

4. This understanding of revelation, which conceives of it as appealing to the human being by way of signs, respects – and indeed helps to make clearer – the best findings in recent philosophical reflection. Christian realism can be reformulated in terms of what has been called a 'symbolic ontology'. And an ontology conceived along such lines is capable of rethinking both the modality of being's self-communication and the nexus between truth and freedom. Although we cannot here attempt a detailed exposition, we shall simply observe that this ontology provides an account of being as a mystery to which we cannot have access but which manifests itself in the contingent sign, and so reveals itself by appealing to the subject to which it is directed, thus allowing the human subject freely to acknowledge or assent to it.[87] The manifestation and communication of being is always mediated through the sign; and in this way, it appeals to the conscience of one who would receive it. In his assent to being, a man's freedom necessarily concurs with his reason, otherwise it would follow that man fabricates the meaning of being on the basis of an unthinking decision. Man cannot come to know, exclusively by his own initiative, what is the fulfilment of the call that has been directed toward him. Of necessity, he acknowledges himself as called and surprised by a correspondence; so too, he is moved to adhere to that which beckons him; and through his adherence, the substance of the call will be revealed to him. Balthasar shows how every act of human knowledge involves this structure, because man can neither resolve nor surpass the difference between the mystery and the sign.[88]

From the sacramental nature of the incarnation it therefore

follows that when a man experiences something of the fullness of his life, he verifies historically the truth of Christ's
promise that he will receive 'a hundred times more now in
this present age, with persecutions, and in the age to come,
eternal life'.[89] Christian revelation is in profound agreement
with the dynamic of man's historical constitution, which
adheres to the truth in and through every aspect of reality.
For it animates that dynamic, by provoking us to a fuller and
more satisfactory exercise of our freedom and reason. Thus
the Christian method is not merely to inculcate some dis-
course; it does not merely counterpose to some system of ideas
an alternate system; still less does it require submission to
the irrational dictates of some power external to one's conscience. It is the verification of a proposal that affects all
aspects of a person's life and all dimensions of reality,[90] on the
basis of the undeniable correspondence awakened by his
encounter with Christ and his Church, who have become for
him an interlocutor. In this way, human responsibility is
exalted, because the mystery itself has made an appeal to the
human being, to which he can, and indeed must, respond,[91] not
only once, or every now and again, but on every occasion, in
all instances of life, all of which is made clear in light of the
great sign that is the incarnation of the word and the gift of
the Holy Spirit.[92]

Mgr Giussani accords extraordinary educational weight to
the category of 'verification' precisely in order to rescue the
reasonableness of the Christian claim.

> The Church proposes to enter into the drama of the uni-
> versal comparison to which man is projected when he paral-
> lels any element of reality with the elementary experience
> constituting his heart. The challenge the Church launches
> can be summarized in this way: it bets on man, so to speak,
> hypothesizes that the message which it brings will be sifted
> by man's elementary experience and will reveal the won-
> drous presence.[93]

Mary is the perfect example of what we have called the
'anthropological focus' of the Church. In her we see the para-

digmatic constitution of the Christian personality, which is why she indicates the privileged method of the incarnation. Mgr Giussani's teaching has always drawn from, and pointed to, the figure of the Virgin; but in the most recent period, his vision of the Christian and of the reality of the Church displays a genuinely 'Mariological focus', evident, for example, in his comments on Dante's 'Hymn to the Virgin'.[94]

Giussani contemplates the mystery of the Virgin Mary, and in her 'the necessary method to have a familiarity with Christ'.[95] If every man reaches happiness when he recognizes and acknowledges reality all the way to its mysterious origin in Christ, one can say that the supreme drama of human freedom is that being has asked that it be recognized and acknowledged. We are all called to live this adherence to the mystery by way of an impact with reality so attractive that we can describe this adherence as a new creation, given by the Father. In the Virgin Mary, says Giussani, this adherence 'becomes a being moved by the Infinite [which is why] the figure of the Virgin is the realization of the Christian personality'.[96] This unlimited or unconditional capacity to embrace the real, which identifies Mary's stance in the world, shows Mary's absolute and trusting surrender to God's plans, by responding with her *Fiat* to the message of the angel. That is why it can be said that 'the Virgin totally respected the freedom of God, she "saved" his freedom; she obeyed God because she respected His freedom without imposing her own method'.[97]

Mary has been kept free from sin by her own Immaculate Conception, and has realized the fullness of her humanity because she enjoys the privilege of her Assumption, body and soul, into heaven. In her, Giussani sees the full image of the destiny to which we are all called (the new Eve). But she not only points to the goal; she also shows the way. The superabundance of the mystery's self-communication has encountered, in Mary's freedom, an availability so great that in her the gratuitous adherence to the designs of God have allowed her to live virginity – that is to say, a relationship with things and persons that is truly adequate to them, a relationship that Giussani defined as 'possession that contains within it a distance'.[98] And it is in just that way that Christ dealt with the whole of reality. Here is the core of a true fertility, of a true maternity, which expands outward from her Son to include all whom Jesus on the cross entrusted to her, through the mediation of the beloved disciple.[99] We have every right to say that Mary is the image of the Church, as Vatican II teaches us. She is the mother of all Christians, efficacious intercessor before her Son.[100]

This anthropological and ecclesial sensitivity, and its Marian focus, finds its simplest and effective expression in the short prayer, *Veni Sancte Spiritus, veni per Mariam!* – a prayer Giussani recommended that one repeat as often as possible each day.[101] In it one can see the luminous assurance that the regenerative power of the Holy Spirit can penetrate hearts, as *lux beatissima* and raging fire, ardent so that man can be a real protagonist in his own life and in the world. The communication of the Spirit occurs through the flesh of Mary/Church.

Education and mission in daily life

Bearing in mind the difficulties we face in our current situation, but also, above all, the nature of the Church as an event encountered, according to a sacramental method, in time and in space, we conclude by offering a few suggestions about Christian education.

Education implies that one follow another

A Christian education is only possible as 'discipleship'. If Christ is the living truth, it is impossible to separate the 'what' from the 'how' of his teaching or proposal. One can only assent to that which he teaches by following him as a disciple. Thanks to the fact the disciples lived their lives in an enduring personal relationship with Jesus, whom they followed from town to town throughout Palestine, they came to know themselves, the true face of God and the destiny of the whole world. Because they lived with him, they could ask him questions about the things he said and did. They watched him pray, they saw how he dealt with people and evaluated events, they accepted his correction, they saw him give up his life on the cross. And in this way they assimilated, as if by osmosis, the unified and unifying standpoint from which he regarded all aspects of life, and his criteria for judging them. In discipleship one learns the truth from a living point of departure.[102] Discipleship is in reality a coessential dimension of Christian faith, without which one can neither attain an understanding of the truth nor live in its light. Far more than a mere condition for the possibility of something other than it, discipleship is, one could say, both in and of itself the beginning of our salvation.

Personal and collective witness
In order that discipleship be possible, there must be someone to follow. That is why personal and communitarian 'witness' is determinative for Christian education. For in a very concrete way, the witness brings a person closer to the dynamism of the living ecclesial tradition, by putting him before the human sign of the mystery, who then asks him to respond, in freedom, with a decision. Through the witness, Christ calls man to a free adherence to him. The deed of witnessing constitutes a gratuitous fact, which leaves a man's freedom intact, without, however, leaving him indifferent, because witness is provocative, it awakens in one's heart a surprising and familiar correspondence. The witness moves a person, it sets him on his way. But he also walks with the person along his journey, a journey on which human reason and human freedom are exercised more fully each day. Precisely because it is inherent in the character of witnessing that it be recognized as such by the person who encounters the witness, man's freedom is, in an exquisite fashion, saved from all imposition or presumption, since it is the person who notices with surprise that a curiosity has been awakened in him, which leads him to desire for himself what he sees realized in the other.[103] In this sense, the witness is truly an authoritative teacher, because that which he communicates so persuasively he has made his own. Because his teaching has so clearly changed his own life,

because it has manifestly given him a new affection for things and rendered him able to judge things in a new way, the teacher shows by his very life that what he teaches is useful to himself, and so also to the student, and indeed to any human being. That is why 'the witness of a Christian life is the first and irreplaceable form of mission: Christ, whose mission we continue, is the "witness" *par excellence* (Rev. 1.5; 3.14) and the model of all Christian witness'.[104]

Verifying the testimony

Christian discipleship both requires and permits personal 'verification' of the testimony. In living their everyday lives in the company of Jesus, the disciples acquired ever more profound reasons to be with him. Their lived experience with Jesus revealed its internal reasonableness in such a way that as time went by, their conviction was affirmed: 'This is it!' In a similar manner, the believer today discovers, in the measure that he lives the faith, that his humanity is enlarged according to a measure that surpasses by far whatever had been predicted that he would make of his life, and whatever he himself might have expected from it. That is to say, he discovers, much to his surprise, that he is more and more himself in all his spheres of activity and interest. In following an Other, he finds that he is beginning to be himself, to be his own 'I'.

Only the verification of testimony within a relationship of discipleship allows one to overcome the after-effects of rationalism: clericalism and dualistic spirituality. It is of capital importance that education be a living discipleship, the following, in one's freedom, of the witness. By the same token, it is essential that such an education be verified, because it is only through the method of verification that the exceptional correspondence or affinity one has recognized in one's first encounter with the witness matures, reaches the point of personal certainty. And as a man proceeds along this path, he will, in turn, himself become a witness; he, too will announce to others what he has heard, what he has seen with his own eyes, what he has looked at and touched with his own hands. A man who finds himself in the company of the witness, and who tests for himself what is announced to him, begins to grow in reasons that sustain a human certainty. Faith shows its credibility, therefore, as a dimension internal to its own itinerary.

Permanent openness to, and engagement with, reality
A Christian education lived as a following or discipleship, with all of the features we have just considered, becomes the place of a permanent openness to, and engagement with, the whole of reality. That is why another sign of a truly effective Christian education is its 'cultural' dimension in the widest sense of the word. It will propose a synthetic point of view from which to look at the world, and become a criterion for learning to evaluate everything and hold fast to what is good.[105] In this way, Christian education perfects the ideal of any genuine education. For with a gaze that is truly ecumenical, such an education will foster the total realization of the person through an openness to all dimensions of reality.

An educational process with these features does not interrupt the transmission of that which it has received, but rather increases it by adding to it the wealth of its own store. In this way, the education of the Christian person will contribute to the perpetuation of the Christian fact as a living tradition: a tradition that rises up to greet every human being with the promise of a happiness that is lacking in nothing, the realization of which is already rationally apparent in the transformed humanity of the witness whom the believer follows with affection. Throughout the course of his life, such a person will walk with hope, until the day that the loving face of the mystery reveals itself forever.

Prayer
The abiding stance of the believer during his earthly life is prayer. In a memorable speech delivered before John Paul II, Giussani recalled that

> human freedom, in which the Mystery is always implicated, has as its supreme and unassailable form of expression the

act of prayer. This is why freedom poses itself, in accordance with the full truth of its nature, as an entreaty to adhere to Being, therefore to Christ. Even in his incapacity, even in his great weakness, man's affection for Christ is destined to endure ... It is for this reason that existence expresses itself, as ultimate ideal, in begging. The real protagonist of history is the beggar: Christ who begs for man's heart, and man's heart that begs for Christ.[106]

Notes

1. I want to express my gratitude to Esmeralda Negrón and John C. McCarthy, who translated this essay.
2. John Paul II, *Ecclesia in Europa* [*EE*], 47; see also 7 and ff.
3. *EE* also acknowledges yet another aspect of the question whose importance cannot be underestimated: many Europeans have never truly heard Christ proclaimed, and for such people not a re-evangelization but an entirely new evangelization is needed. The apostolic exhortation refers, in a general way, to countries in central and Eastern Europe that have recently emerged from communist rule, but also to the children of emigrants who profess other religions. For this reason, Europe is to be considered a continent of mission *ad gentes* (46).
4. Cf. *EE*, 7–9.
5. L. Giussani, *Why the Church?* (Montreal, Kingston, London and Ithaca NY: McGill–Queen's University Press, 2001). My reading of this text will be amplified by occasional references to the chapters added to the most recent Italian edition, *Perché la Chiesa?* (Milan: Rizzoli, 2003); I shall also cite other works by Giussani in the course of this essay.
6. See, in particular, the contributions by Cardinals Bergoglio, O'Connor, Ouellet, Stafford and Scola, as also those by Albacete, Brague, Lobkowicz, Schindler, Waldstein, in the recent collection edited by E. Buzzi, *A Generative Thought. An Introduction to the Works of Luigi*

Giussani (Montreal and Kingston–London–Ithaca: McGill–Queen's University Press, 2003).

7. On this point see A. Scola, 'Christ, the Light of the Nations: The Church, His Spouse and Helpmate', a paper presented at 'The Call to Holiness and Communion: Vatican Council II on the Church', a conference held at the John Paul II Cultural Center, in Washington, DC, 12–14 November 2003. And by the same author, 'La Logica dell'incarnazione come logica sacramentale', in *Wer ist die Kirche?* (Freiburg: Johannes Verlag Einsiedeln, 1999), pp. 99–135.

8. J.H. Newman, *Essay in Aid of a Grammar of Assent* (London and New York: Longmans, 1903), pp. 55–7. What the English cardinal warned about in his era has been denounced in our century by the great biblical scholar H. Schlier, when he observes, 'a growing distance, an estrangement between common thinking and Christian faith . . . [F]or public and general sensitivity, fundamental Christian terms and their meaning have become, in great measure, incomprehensible'.

9. See the story in M. Camisasca, *Comunione e liberazione. Volume I: Le Origini (1954–1968)* (Cinisello Balsamo: San Paolo, 2001), p. 94.

10. L. Giussani, *L'Uomo e il suo destino in cammino* (Genoa: Marietti, 1999), p. 133.

11. Ibid., pp. 133–143. The five 'withouts' are, respectively: God without Christ, Christ without the Church, the Church without the world, the world without the I, the I without God.

12. G.K. Chesterton, *The Autobiography* (New York: Sheed & Ward, 1936). See especially the end of Chapter 7.

13. Cf. *Lumen Gentium*, Chapter 1: 'The Mystery of the Church'. See also Scola, 'Christ, the Light of the Nations'.

14. This is not the place to offer a detailed explanation of what it means to say that the Church is, evidently, a social reality, visibly recognizable and organized in its institutional and hierarchical elements. As is obviously the case, the 'supernatural character' of this grouping of human beings

must be underlined; one must understand that the Church is, from the beginning, a mystery above all else. Regarding the description of these aspects of the life of the Church, see Giussani, *Why the Church?*, pp. 72–111; 163–200.

15. That the Church should be conceived in this way inevitably entails that one views participation in its life in terms of representative democracy, with all of the complications that always arise from this type of association.

16. Cf. Jn 1.35–51; Mt. 9.9.

17. Giussani, *Perché la Chiesa?*, p. v.

18. See the original description of the nature of the Christian encounter in L. Giussani, *At the Origin of the Christian Claim* (Montréal, Kingston, London and Ithaca, NY: McGill–Queen's University Press, 1998), pp. 36–48. Also L. Giussani, S. Alberto, and J. Prades, *Generare tracce nella storia del mondo* (Milan: Rizzoli, 2001), pp. 5–28.

19. The great Latin theologians from Augustine through to Anselm and Thomas Aquinas all consistently affirm the incomprehensible nature of the mystery of God, and so establish as classical a teaching that is dogmatically ratified in, among other canonical texts, the Fourth Lateran Council (DH 806) and the First Vatican Council (DH 3001).

20. Cf. Giussani, *Why the Church?*, pp. 103–4.

21. J.H. Newman, *An Essay on the Development of Christian Doctrine* (Westminster, MD: Christian Classics, 1968), p. 3.

22. R. Guardini provides some lucid reflections regarding the historical character of revelation, which is the way in which God himself has sought to communicate with the world, although he could have done so in many other ways. Cf. 'Revelación e historia', in A. Robert Caponigri (ed.), *Pensadores católicos contemporáneos* (Barcelona: Grijalbo, 1964), Vol. 2 pp. 247–61.

23. T.S. Eliot, *Choruses from 'The Rock'*, VII: *The Complete*

Poems and Plays of T.S. Eliot (London and Boston, MA: Faber and Faber, 1985), p. 160.

24. See Giussani, *Why the Church?*, pp. 11–17.
25. A still more significant case of the modern domestication of Christianity than Kant's is Hegel's. To provide a proper account of the development of the problem of the secularization of Christianity would, however, exceed the bounds of the present discussion. For a fuller discussion of the issue, see my ' "Eius dulcis Praesentia". Notas sobre el acceso del hombre al misterio de Dios', *Revista española de teologia* 62 (2002): 5–44; see also my *Dios ha salvado la distancia* (Madrid: Encuentro, 2003), which includes bibliographical references.
26. *Veritatis Splendor* 25: 'Christ's contemporaneity for people of all times is shown forth in his body, which is the Church.' See also *Lumen Gentium*, 14 and *CCC*, 556, 1085.
27. *EE*, 22.
28. The word 'Church' indicates an historical phenomenon whose only meaning lies in the fact that it enables man to attain a certainty about Christ ... If we think that we have the option not to assume a personal position concerning the historical fact of Christ, then the interest that the Church has for our lives will only be reduced to the level of sociological or political problem or a problem of association to be fought for or defended. (Giussani, *Why the Church?*, pp. 8–9)

29. Ibid., p. 119.
30. Ibid., p. 123.
31. J.H. Newman, *Apologia pro vita sua* (London: Oxford University Press, 1964), pp. 337–8.
32. C. Péguy, *The Portal of the Mystery of Hope*, trans. D.L. Schindler, Jr (Grand Rapids, MI: Eerdmans, 1996), pp. 59–60, cited with comments in Giussani, *Why the Church?*, p. 127.
33. Cf. *DH*, 302.
34. *Why the Church?*, p. 20.

35. Ibid.
36. Giussani describes and critically evaluates each position, ibid., pp. 11–20.
37. Lk. 10.16.
38. Cf. Jn 14.12; Jn 5.20.
39. Jn 15.5.
40. 1 Cor. 10.17; Eph. 4.25.
41. 1 Jn 1.1–3
42. Lk. 22.19.
43. Here would be the place to develop some reflections about the seven sacraments, beginning with baptism, which is the origin and the source of Christian life, in conjunction with the eucharist (cf. *Why the Church?*, pp. 183–9).
44. Pope John Paul II clearly points to this character of the Church in his 'Letter to the Revd Mgr L. Giussani on the twentieth anniversary of the recognition of the Fraternity [of Communion and Liberation] by the Pontifical Council for the Laity':

> The Movement, therefore, has chosen and chooses to indicate not *a* road, but *the* road toward a solution to this existential drama [of man]. The road, as you have affirmed so many times, is Christ. He is the Way, the Truth, and the Life, who reaches the person in his day-to-day existence. The discovery of this road normally comes about through the mediation of other human beings. Marked through the gift of faith by the encounter with the Redeemer, believers are called to become an echo of the event of Christ, to become them-selves an 'event'. (*Traces* 3 [2002])

45. *CCC* no. 515.
46. Preface to Nativity I. See also: 'In the holy mystery that we celebrate today, Christ the Lord, without leaving the glory of the Father, makes himself present among us in a new way: the one that was invisible by his nature makes himself visible by adopting our nature; the eternal, begot-ten before time, shares our temporary life . . .' (Preface to Nativity, II).

47. Irenaeus of Lyon, *Adversus haereses*, IV, 20, 5.

48. Ephraem of Nisibis, *Himno de nativitate* IV. Cf. F.J. Martínez, 'Jesús y María en algunos himnos de Efrén de Nísibe', *Estudios Marianos* 64 (1998): 203–53. E. Beck, *Des heiligen Ephraem des Syrers Hymnen de Fide* (Louvain, 1955 = CSCO 155).

49. Augustine, *Tracts on the First Letter of Saint John* 1, 1 (PL 35: 1978).

50. 'Illud videtur esse convenientissimum ut per visibilia monstretur invisibilia Dei': *Summa Theologiae* III q. 1. a. 1 sc.

51. Cf. Giussani, *Perché la Chiesa*, V, 135, 244, 307.

52. *Adv. Haer.* IV, 20, 7.

53. Cf. Mt. 1.23.

54. Cf. Jn 1.18; 1 Tim. 1.17.

55. Cf. Lk. 1.32.

56. Cf. Augustine, *The Confessions* III: 6.

57. Cf. H.U. von Balthasar, *Gloria*, Vol. I (Madrid: Encuentro, 1985), p. 141. St Thomas had already given classical expression to this thought with the expression 'forma dat esse'.

58. Cf. H.U. von Balthasar, *Teológica*, Vol. I (Madrid: Encuentro, 1997), pp. 153ff.

59. Jn 14.9; 12.45.

60. Balthasar, *Gloria*, Vol. 1, p. 158.

61. Cf. *Lumen Gentium*, 8 and 12.

62. Cf. J. Carrón, 'La Permanencia de la experiencia cristiana en el libro de los Hechos', *Communio* (Spanish edn), 18 (1996): 270–84.

63. This is not to say that there is complete identity between the Church and Christ, since the Church is not only his body but also his wife, who awaits his return (cf. Rev. 22.20); even so, in her the Lord certainly lives.

64. See the precise formula in *Gaudium et Spes*, 21: 'to make God the Father and His Incarnate Son present and in a sense visible . . .'

65. Cf. H. de Lubac. *Catolicismo* (Madrid: Encuentro, 1988), pp. 37–56.

66. *Dei Verbum*, 2. The implications of this sacramental structure of revelation for education in the faith and catechesis
have been broached by Mgr Giussani in 'The Method of a
Presence', *Traces* 1 (2003): 41.

67. Given that this is not the place to elaborate upon this
development, I shall simply refer to 'Messaggio di Giovanni Paolo II' in *I Movimenti nella Chiesa. Atti del
Congresso mondiale dei movimenti ecclesiali (Roma, 27–
29 maggio 1998)* (Vatican City: Libreria Editrice Vaticana, 1999), pp. 13–19 and 219–24. Cf. also Giussani *et
al.*, *Generare Tracce*, pp. 107–15. J. Ratzinger, 'I Movimenti ecclesiali e la loro collocazione teologica', in *I
Movimenti nella Chiesa*, pp. 23–51. A. Scola, 'La Realtà
dei movimenti nella Chiesa universale e nella chiesa
locale', in *I Movimenti nella Chiesa*, pp. 105–27. And L.
Gerosa, *Carisma e diritto nella Chiesa* (Milan: Jaca,
1989).

68. It goes without saying that our attempt to lay certain
theological foundations does not eliminate the necessity of
providing, on another occasion, a full and precise account
of the doctrinal and moral reasoning that bears upon the
controversial themes we have merely mentioned. Suffice
it to say, however, that such a task would be made far
easier were the context for such a discussion a lived and
joyful experience of ecclesial belonging to Christ, which is
our concern here.

69. Cf. Jn 1.39. We might here recall Newman's celebrated
distinction between real and notional assent, for which
see the *Grammar of Assent*, pp. 36–97. The dogmatic
Constitution *Dei Verbum* (5) has effectively underscored
the integral character of the act of faith in Christological
revelation.

70. Cf. Mt. 19.25.

71. Cf. *Veritatis Splendor*, 19. Also Giussani *et al.*, *Generare
tracce*, pp. 144–56.

72. 'Cum cognovimus Christum, viri efficimur et iam non
parvuli', *In epist. ad Ephesios*, II, 4, v. 14 in *Marii Victorini
Opera exegetica* Vol. 2 (Vienna, 1986), p. 16.

73. This is not to deny that there are doctrinal and moral statements that are accesible to human intelligence solely by the light of natural reason. All the same, let us recall, with the First Vatican Council, that even as regards truths that are immediately accessible to reason (in our present historical condition) supernatural revelation is *morally* necessary: cf. *DH* 3005 (and *DH* 3876).

74. Eliot, *Choruses from 'The Rock'*, IX, and X, pp. 165, 167.

75. Giussani, *Why the Church?*, p. 192.

76. Cf. L. Giussani, *L'Autocoscienza del cosmo* (Milan: Rizzoli, 2000), pp. 291–363; *Affezione e dimora* (Milan: Rizzoli, 2001), pp. 47–9; 243–99, 347.

77. *Why the Church?*, p. 190.

78. For a more ample analysis of the characteristics of a faith that lovingly acknowledges the gift that is the presence of Christ, as presented in certain other texts of Mgr Giussani, see my 'The Christian: Subject of a New Culture', in E. Buzzi (ed.), *A Generative Thought*, pp. 113–27.

79. Cf. Giussani, *Perché la Chiesa?*, p. 307. The very incomprehensibility of the mystery, so contrary to all rationalistic or semi-rationalistic tendencies, is not dissolved by this statement, since, as Giussani also writes in this text, 'arriving at the end of the road, when everything ought finally to be clear, we will find ourselves obligated to recognize that everything is Mystery. That is why it will appear that words and arguments lack verifiability if it is not acknowledged that at the end of all things God emerges with power before our eyes as Mystery', p. v.

80. Giussani, *Why the Church?*, p. 184.

81. L. Giussani, *L'Uomo e il suo destino*, pp. 128–9.

82. Ibid., pp. 131ff. In the same place Cardinal Ratzinger is cited as acknowledging that 'Only God, by making himself finite, in order to shatter our finitude and lead it to its infinite dimension, is able to satisfy all the needs of our being.' Further on, there appears a very interesting explanation of the similarity and radical difference

between the religious sense that is the defining mark of human nature and Christian faith. G.K. Chesterton realized straightaway that the encounter with the Church stimulates the capacity for reason: 'A thinking man can think himself deeper and deeper into Catholicism . . . conversion is the beginning of an active, fruitful, progressive and even adventurous life of the intellect.' (See *The Thing* [New York: Sheed & Ward, 1929], p. 212.)

83. See the numerous comments by Giussani regarding the delicate interplay between appearances and being, and between the concrete circumstances of life and the mystery who reveals himself in Jesus Christ: *The Religious Sense* (Montréal–Kingston–Buffalo: McGill–Queen's University Press, 1997), pp. 110–24. *L'Autocoscienza del cosmo*, pp. 208–9; 295–7; 'Being is Charity', *Traces* 10 (2002): 45.

84. We may find a certain kinship with the epistemology of J.H. Newman and his famous doctrine of antecedent probabilities. Cf. *Fifteen Sermons Preached before the University of Oxford* (London: SPCK, 1970), especially the tenth and eleventh sermons, pp. 176–221.

85. For a more detailed elaboration of this notion, see Giussani, *Why the Church?*, pp. 189–95 and *L'Uomo e il suo destino, passim.*

86. C.S. Lewis, *A Grief Observed* (London: Faber and Faber, 1966), pp. 17, 55–6.

87. For an explanation of this term and its theoretical significance see the works cited in note 25.

88. Von Balthasar, *Teológica*, Vol. I, p. 173.

89. Cf. Mk 10.30.

90. Cf. *Why the Church?*, pp. 154–5.

91. Cf. Lk. 2.34–35. Giussani insists that a man's basic stance towards reality is revealed in the attitude he takes with regard to the Church: does he love the truth more than himself, or does he prefer himself to the extent that he allows the truth to pass him by? Cf. *Why the Church?*, pp. 136–41.

92. Cf. *Gaudium et Spes*, 22.

93. *Why the Church?*, p. 204. See the entirety of Chapter 9: 'The Locus of Verification: Human Experience' (pp. 203–9). We will deal with the educational implications of this category below.

94. See, among others, the following texts, which were either addressed to the members of the Movement Communion and Liberation or published in the Italian press over the last 12 months or so: 'Moved by the Infinite. Letter to the Fraternity of Communion and Liberation': *Traces* 7 (2003): 1–3; 'Message for the Pilgrimage Macerata–Loreto': *Traces* 7 (2003) 41; 'Oboedientia et pax': *Traces* 10 (2003): 1–2; 'Letter to the Holy Father': *Traces* 10 (2003): 49; '*Sopra la 'ruina*': *Traces* 11 (2003): 1–3; 'Simplicity, Docile Daughter of Happiness': *Traces* 2 (2004): 1–3; 'Our Indestructible Company': *Avvenire* (24 December 2003), p. 1. To these we should add the new chapter included in the most recent Italian edition of *Why the Church?*, which is dedicated to the Virgin Mary (pp. 307–10). In every one of these texts, Mgr Giussani takes clear inspiration from St Bernard's Hymn to the Virgin, which Dante included in the *Divine Comedy* (*Paradise* XXXIII) (Milan: Rizzoli, 2001), pp. 389ff. All texts are available from the international website of Communion and Liberation: www.comunioneliberazione.org/

95. 'Moved by the Infinite'.

96. Ibid.

97. Ibid.

98. Cf. Giussani, *Affezione e dimora*, p. 250.

99. Cf. Jn 19.25–27.

100. Cf. *Lumen Gentium*: Chapter 8.

101. Cf. L. Giussani, *Tutta la terra desidera il tuo volto* (Cinisello Balsamo: Paoline, 2000), pp. 206–8.

102. This shows how in Christian life the content of the faith and human experience are properly united, and so able to overcome the ruptures between theory and praxis that have so frequently plagued modern pedagogy. Cf. *General Directory for Catechesis* (1997), 67.

103. The Church Fathers were always conscious that the

divine initiative proceeded '*non cum vi . . . sed secundum suadelam*' (Irenaeus, *Adv. haer.* V, 1, 1).

104. *Redemptoris Missio*, 42.
105. Cf. 1 Thess. 5.21.
106. 'In the Simplicity of my Heart I have gladly given You everything' (Fr Giussani's testimony during the meeting of the Holy Father John Paul II with the ecclesial movements and the new communities, St Peter's Square. Rome, 30 May 1998).

5

The Meaning of the Organism of Attachments for the Church's Evangelization

Bryan Cunningham

Introduction

Much has been said in earlier chapters about the context of evangelization for the Church in the modern world. Therefore, in the first part of this chapter I will deal with just some of the indicators which help to mark out the task(s) of evangelization today. In so doing, I will draw to a great extent on the report by Philip Knights and Andrea Murray, *Evangelisation in England and Wales*.[1] I will then go on to consider the work of Fr Josef Kentenich, founder of the Schönstatt Community, and his insight into the subject of evangelization.

Youth

The diversity of personality types, tastes and the mystery of being human are as rich among contemporary young people as they are amongst any other generation. Many choices exist today and many choices are made: there is therefore not a single youth culture. That being said we should note some trends. There is a post-secular trend: spirituality, mystery, non-empirical and aesthetic desires and even ritual are often seen as positive things. Some young people value community and a strong framework within which to live. But one frequently meets significant distrust of authorities and institutions: this is often expressed in terms of individualism and a sense of the right to make personal choices. This leads to a high degree of moral relativism and an emphasis on personal pleasure. There is also a high degree of moral indignation, not least about environmental issues and the destructive potential of global capitalism.

Some young people display powerful and passionate commitments, even while many of their peers seem to be apathetic and without any focus. Many young people are happily exploring the possibilities of new technologies; others show a technophobic suspicion. Some of these trends may appear paradoxical but their very variety underlines the point that many options are open to youth cultures which are likely to become ever more pluralistic and amorphous. Both 'yob culture' and World Youth Day in Rome in the Holy Year 2000 are actual, if contradictory, contemporary expressions of youth cultures.[2]

Marriage and family life

'The family in the modern world, as much as and perhaps more than any other institution, has been beset by the many profound and rapid changes that have affected society and culture' (*Familiaris Consortio*). *Evangelisation 2002* goes on to say:

> We have also witnessed major changes in marriage and family life. Patterns of unmarried cohabitation, children born outside marriage, marriage breakdown, children brought up with one parent, remarriage after divorce and children brought up with step-parents are common and coexist alongside more traditional and, for the Church more comfortable, patterns of marriages and families.[3]

Alternative lifestyles

The study continues:

> Likewise there is increasing social acceptance of a range of lifestyles, sexualities and non-traditional forms of families, including same-sex relationships. People today experience a wide range of role-models as to how to form relationships and how to raise children. This social reality is within the Catholic community as well as a trend in the general population.[4]

Issues of gender equality and political correctness
Contemporary society has made substantial gains in promoting the dignity of women, so that women play a more central role in economics, politics and in society in general. In the wake of this development has come a whole series of 'awarenesses', most of which fall under the title of 'inclusive society'. A downside of these developments can occur when such developments in connection with a more pragmatic political correctness lead to moral relativism and can even invert and become exclusive and absolute.[5]

Modernity and postmodernism
Woolly terms for woolly times! To late modernity belong trends expressed in individualism, materialism, economism and secularism. The end of the 'great stories' such as Marxism, the demise of overarching authorities and ideologies, eclecticism and recurring impermanence leading to a basic inability to make long-term decisions can be considered as characteristics of the postmodern era.[6] We live in a multi-options society which realizes Andy Warhol's prediction of 15 minutes of fame or notoriety for everyone, for which purpose we now have academies.

The Church: from museum-piece to soul of the world
In terms of a new context there is a chance that the Church could be reduced to vestigial relics of former glory. It would have the relevance of the anachronism of the Beefeaters of the Tower: Westminster or Canterbury being wonderful examples of medieval architecture. There is already the danger of the Church and Church opinion being marginalized, disqualified as an uncomfortable vociferous minority. At present we have the long debate on the new European constitution and whether the Christian roots of what we now call Europe – previously it was called Christendom – can be affirmed in that document. How do we as Church relate to the world, and what do we see as the task of evangelization in this context?

The role of the Christian in society

In the Letter to Diognetus[7] we have a fine example of the role of the Christian in society and the relationship of the Church to the world. To summarize: what the soul is to the body, so Christians are in the world. Just as the soul is dispersed through all the members of the body, so Christians are scattered through all the cities of the world.

The role of the Church in the modern world

Evangelization means that the Church takes up its role as soul of the new, developing world.

> For the Church, evangelization means bringing the Good News into all strata of humanity, and through its influence transforming humanity from within and making it new . . . for the Church it is a question not only of preaching the Gospel in ever wider geographic areas or to ever greater numbers of people, but also of affecting and as it were upsetting, through the power of the Gospel, mankind's criteria of judgement, determining values, points of interest, lines of thought, sources of inspiration and models of life, which are in contrast with the Word of God and the plan of salvation.
>
> All this could be expressed in the following words: what matters is to evangelize man's culture and cultures (not in a purely decorative way, as it were, by applying a thin veneer, but in a vital way, in depth and right to [its] very roots) in the wide and rich sense which these terms have in *Gaudium et Spes* (50), always taking the person as [the] starting-point and always coming back to the relationships of people among themselves and with God.[8]

What is meant by the term 'organism of attachments'?

For Fr Josef Kentenich, founder of the Schönstatt Community, the term 'organism of attachments' implies the networking of life in relationships in the natural and the supernatural order. In the natural order it embraces persons, things, places and ideas. In 1930, in considering the concept of attachment as central to his approach to education and psychology, he saw that this network encompasses the person to whom there is a significant attachment: his home, his work and his vision of the world. Central to Kentenich's understanding and experience was the development of attachments as personal bonds of the soul, rooted emotionally in the core of the person. Correspondingly, the organism of attachments configures within a whole organism which is only complete when the world of heaven, particularly in the relationship to the triune God and to Mary, is included. It was central to Kentenich's thinking that faith could only really grow within the context of true human development. He was convinced that the only way to evangelize in the modern world was to develop the double organism of attachments in a healthy way.

Since the 1950s the term 'attachment' is associated with John Bowlby and his theory of attachment. Lee A. Kirkpatrick writes,

> Although Bowlby's theorizing about attachment focused largely on the evolutionary origins of the attachment system and its manifestations in infant–mother relationships, he clearly believed from the beginning that the processes and dynamics of attachment have broad implications for social development and psychological functioning across the lifespan.[9]

Kirkpatrick goes on to say that there are many aspects of religious belief and behaviour which can be meaningfully and usefully interpreted in terms of attachment dynamics. When Kentenich uses the term, he is of course not restricting himself to the dynamics of a psychological process. He is referring to real relationships which transcend the natural order and encompass the invisible supernatural order.

Thus the term is used here in a broader sense than Bowlby's. It is, however, interesting that Kirkpatrick explains that the dynamics of Bowlby's attachment process can be seen in religious responses as adults: seeking and maintaining the proximity of God – virtually all religions provide places where one can be closer to God; God as a haven of safety – many turn to God in times of crises and distress (here prayer plays an important role in religious attachment behaviour); and God as a secure base – with God as my rock, my shield, I develop a confident, self-assured approach to life. Also the notion of separation from God is one of the better definitions of hell and damnation.[10]

The need for a change in mindset

The organism of attachments can only be correctly perceived in a mindset of organic thinking as opposed to mechanistic thinking. Prerequisite to building this network of attachments in an organic way is this change in mindset.[11]

Mechanistic thinking

Mechanistic thinking is a notion describing the separation of worlds which belong together. A classic example is when God is literally taken out of the picture. One of my favourite examples comes from the time I was studying the history of science. When Isaac Newton discovered the concept of angular momentum to explain why the planets remained in their orbits, the angels who had been doing the job until then were made redundant. The ongoing secularization during the Enlightenment and after, meant that God was less and less necessary to explain and support the physics of the world.

One of the results of this mechanical separation was the loss of the context of the secondary mediator between the Creator and his creation. Many aspects of life, which had been net-worked together, and were seen in a context of belonging together, now lost that framework. Marriage was seen in its intrinsic human value, and the notion of a real symbol of the relationship between Christ and his Church was lost. The world of work outgrew the notions binding creativity and self-realization within the context of a loving and caring Creator. The more the analytical approach to the world and the use of the empirical methods to understanding our world became a mentality, the more the tendency to separate and divide –

literally dissect – an organic whole into separate, autonomous parts. Mechanistic thinking, according to Kentenich, has been the predominant form of thinking which has created a mind-set in modernity which separates God from creation (primary and secondary causes). It divides idea from life, and therefore prefers to use abstract concepts estranged from life. Mechanistic thinking atomizes life, life-processes and life-forms. It prepares the way for a multifaceted impersonalization: it depersonalizes God and the human person and our perception of self. It separates one idea from another, and within the human person it separates the capacities of thinking, will and feeling. It leads to a dysfunctional way of life. At one point Kentenich describes mechanistic thinking as the sickness of our time.[12]

Organic thinking
When looking for a way to overcome such a mentality, it is important to find a way of looking at the world which sees all its aspects and dimensions in the context of the whole organism of attachments and their interconnectedness. We have to gain a new perspective in which the love between husband and wife is seen as an expression of their love for God. The way in which parents care and sacrifice for their children and accept the responsibility to educate them within the context of society and the development of a hierarchy of values is to be seen in the context of a God who cares and wants our personal growth. The importance of a world economy which looks towards sustainable growth and development of all peoples, and the advance of technology creating many new possibilities for the improvement of humanity, finds a framework within creation sharing in the creativity of the Creator.

On the level of significance of attachments Kentenich looks towards the quality of the attachments. Many of the problems experienced today are caused by the poor or deficient quality of relationships. The development of an organism of attachment which strives to find a harmony between our attachment to God, the world and the people in our world takes on a formative influence and a determining role in deciding priorities in life. Both of these elements, an organic approach to the world and the quality of the relationships in the organism of attachments, play a central role in the process of evangelization.

Kentenich describes the following characteristics of organic thinking: healthy or wholesome thinking is organic because it sees God and creation together. It is symbolic, forming a bridge between the created world and God. It looks at things in context and does not separate them out of context. It brings ideas together by centring them on core notions of integration. Knowledge should be transformed into love and life,[13] and in this context he says that perception should be *cognitio vitalis* – life-orientated and holistic.[14]

How the organism of attachments works

Natural networking brings about personal commitment and the slow growth of emotionally rooted personal attachments. This occurs between persons. Bowlby teaches us the importance of the development of personal bonds to significant permanent figures in our lives.[15] When this basic attachment fails, the person loses out on the basic trust needed to make them capable of addressing the challenges in their lives. Many psychologists note an increase in schizoid phenomena in modern society, which leads to a basic inability to enter into any long-term relationships. This is of deep significance to the task of evangelization, which requires the need to learn to trust in a loving God. Many skills previously presumed as functionally existent have to be learned. We now have parenting-skills classes to teach adults how to be parents. We have classes in basic socialization teaching children how to relate to others and themselves in an appropriate way. Evangelization can no longer presume 'healthy homes' and 'healthy families', which results in a change of approach and in our means of evangelizing, which has in itself to create these foundation skills and an atmosphere to enable those being evangelized to be receptive.[16]

Network of personal relationships[17]

The organism of attachments seeks to strengthen the bonds among people in a personal way so that these bonds, as significant attachments, have a formative, determining influence on personal growth. This enables those being evangelized to respond in a deep emotional way, so that the growth of faith is anchored in the heart of the person. The interplay of the natural and supernatural order and the attachments to persons in the natural and supernatural worlds are essential to real growth. The backdrop of loving and caring parents forms the experiential basis for the notion of God as Good Shepherd looking after those whom he loves. The transfer of the warm intimacy between child and parents to God as Father, Jesus as a brother and friend as well as Saviour and Lord, and the Spirit as the love I feel for others, is the context in which deep-rooted evangelization occurs. One consequence of this is that the Church has to orientate its growth more towards the model of family.[18]

A counter-indication of healthy growth can be observed when a person isolates himself from the reality of human relationships and uses God as a surrogate or substitute attachment. This happens particularly in cases of severe stress and crisis, grief situations (also psychological loss in separation) and when there has been a history of insecure attachment.[19] Attachment to God in the context of the double organism of attachments is an adequate response, whereas a supernaturalized attachment to God may be a sign of avoidance and denial.

The role of Mary

Central to Kentenich's understanding of the organism of the attachments is the role of Mary. Her role is mother, and as a companion on our journey Mary plays a central part in the connection between natural and supernatural. She helps us to develop the quality of those attachments and the connectedness of our human relationships and our relationship to the divine. Kentenich's anthropological point of departure is

assured of transcendence because it is Marian-based. Relationability of God and his creation remains personal and concrete, and at the same time spiritual and universal, because of
the Marian approach and perspective. Evangelization as a
process finds deeper roots in the notion of instrumentality following faith in divine providence.[20] Essentially we could look
at the various elements of this topic and observe the role of
Mary as a way of concrete realization in a process of growth.

Central to Schönstatt's spirituality is the covenant of love
with Mary. This is a personal bond reflecting the growth of
'perfect devotion' described by Grigion de Montford. The place
where this covenant is enacted both historically (18 October
1914) and as spiritual home is the Shrine to Our Lady of
Schönstatt. In the meantime there is an international network of affiliated shrines. This network of shrines developed
also into a network of personal shrines in the homes of the
members of Schönstatt. The network of the whole organism of
attachments should be based in the heart of our daily lives.
The organism of attachments helps set the context for our
ordinary (secular) life being perceived and understood in their
spiritual, supernatural framework.

Examples in scripture
Biblically we see many examples of the growth of relationship
between persons as the bridging factor for the transmission of
faith. Consider the story of the Samaritan woman at the well.
The deepening of personal relationship and the increase in
personal trust leads to a growing inner revelation of who
Christ is, who plays the foil in this relationship. Raymond E.
Brown tells us that in the literary analysis there are two sub-
divisions in this scene: the one on 'living water', the second on
recognizing who Jesus is in the dialogue on true worship of the
Father.[21] The woman touched to the core of her being by Christ
becomes herself an evangelizer. In terms of the organism of
attachments we recognize that Christ answers in an existential way the needs of the woman: both her need for water and
for salvation. Through the growing relationship she experiences the inner revelation of who stands before her: a Jew, who

is greater than Jacob since he is the giver of living water. Here is a prophet who knows her, and in his giving her understanding without condemnation she recognizes that he is the Christ. The ascent in insight brings with it the commitment to discipleship: she puts down her water-jug, hurries off to the town and encourages others to 'come and see'.

The more we look to the gospels and the letters of the New Testament, the more we find the fundamental role played by building relationships. Following Christ's resurrection, we hear (Acts 2) in the first sermon of Peter the fundamentals of evangelization: *kerygma*, the first in our network of relationships is Christ whose love for us brought him through death to the resurrection; *koinonia*, the challenge to live life in Christ through our attachments to one another; *diakonia*, the basic mode of how the infant Church expressed this life in Christ in their service to one another.

Network of places

Much has been investigated and written about the meaning of home and homelessness for the individual and society. Two key areas for evangelization are the depth-psychological significance of home and the symbolic nature of the experience of home. Home has an effect on the integration of all dimensions of personal emotional receptivity on different levels: irrational, rational and superrational. We could say that we seek the balance of body, heart and soul in the context of home as a symbol of heaven. Our experience of home becomes the place of integration of purified instincts, taken in hand by a strong will and clear mind in the context of a spiritual atmosphere.[22] Our existential need for security finds satisfaction to the extent that home provides such an existential space for us in which we are lovingly accepted and experience safety. This basic experience forms the foundation for a truly anchored religious development.

Experience of home
Home belongs to the deepest of emotional memories for each

person – whether that memory awakens life or brings memories of inhibited life or even suffering. Home has both a personal and local connotation. Whether we like it or not, our home and our experience of home writes major chapters in the biography of us all. When considering this in the perspective of depth-psychological significance, Kentenich quotes frequently the Swiss educationalist Pestalozzi, that each person is a nest-bound being.[23] To be enabled to enter into deeper, more permanent attachments of a truly personal nature we need the experience of home: the place in which we experience security and acceptance. In many ways home is the cradle of self and self-love. Our experience of home also forms the centre of association of all our memories as images and concepts, and becomes the centre of all our feelings and emotions.[24] In so far as we find home in the Church, we find the deepest roots of our being anchored in the place of our faith. Ultimately our home is found in the heart of an ever-loving Father.

The consequence of deficiency
The consequence of deficiency in the experience of home is clear. Christa Meves says that this lack of home experience can lead to total self-neglect.[25] People in our modern world are mobile. Many make the experience of changing, and some of changing often. Particularly in the anonymity of big cities we lose all orientation of being 'earthed'. Some negative results can be clearly charted in the move from more closed cultural systems found often in rural areas or in close-knit communities to the almost limitless possibilities of urban life. People literally no longer know their neighbours, nor do they think they need them. Loss of social control without an increase in personal autonomy demands a greater emotional maturity in order to deal with the challenges. Lack of such growth can lead to total disorientation. In the organism of attachments we have to strengthen the bonds to places of emotional significance: home, school, regular holiday places, parish church. For some, this may also include places of pilgrimage.

Home in three dimensions of meaning

Home has then a physical value, providing as it does our basic needs of shelter, food and growth. Home also has a psychosocial value associated with the psychological and emotional experiences which weave the fabric of our memories. On another level, home has not only its intrinsic value but also a symbolic value which forms the bridge to the supernatural organism of attachments. This essentially describes a metaphysical dimension of home: our earthly home and experience of home is a symbol of our heavenly home and makes us receptive to the values of our spiritual home.[26]

Network of things

A wider context for the network of things is to consider our relationship to the created world. Foremost is the world of work, our feeling of being creative and shaping the destiny and development of the world. Also the possibilities of self-realization belong to the 'things' of the created world. The process of world-development, particularly the social questions and environmental issues, belong to the organism of attachments. Getting the balance right is the task of evangelization in the world.

The modern problem of the world of a thousand disposable things still has influence even in the more environmentally conscious postmodern times. This can illustrate the importance of a comprehensive outlook on the organism of attachments. We can be amazingly inconsistent in our relationship to the world of things. One no-go area has become the child's bedroom. Recent surveys showed the influence that the contents of children's bedrooms can have on the contents policy for house insurance! The economic importance of childhood consumerism is no longer underestimated. On the one hand, we live in the very marvellous world of modern development and have thousands more possibilities than in previous times. On the other hand, the question for healthy human growth and spiritual development lies in finding an organizing principle which emotionally brings order to the expanding cosmos of the world of things. On a second level, we have to ask in the face of overload of worldly things: is the created world a bridge beyond the horizon leading us to the loving Creator, or is it an earthly distraction which, in satisfying lower needs, never allows us to become aware of deeper, more spiritual needs?[27] The world of created things has to become a network of small prophets teaching us of God's presence in our world and God's ways to lead the world (*digitus dei*).

Network of ideas

Important for human beings is the way they look at the world. As we mentioned earlier, the 'great stories' of the last century, such as Marxism, have come to an end. There are systems and ideologies such as communism and capitalism, which are based on false or deformed visions of the world. There ensues a skewed perception of the world. We have to look for the right idea of God, world and humanity. Kentenich looked at truth from the point of view of life. Truth and life belong together. Ideas, which are reality-related, find inner coherence with one another because they allow themselves to be limited to the convergence of being. The integration of truth in life follows through the constant centring of truth and its associated value for life, particularly in the area of religious or theological concepts. Often the reality behind the idea can be forgotten. Kentenich was aware of the dangers of such thinking. He himself bears witness to the fact that there were times when he was so caught up in abstractions and ideas that he could not cope with being involved in personal emotional bonding. The compulsion to think in abstract ideas became a fixation (*Ideenzwang wird Zwangsidee*) and blocked out personal access to the reality and relationability of those realities behind the ideas.[28] So it is not just a question of the dichotomy of theory and practice but rather a perception of reality which separates the concepts from their associated or designated reality. In an extreme scenario, this means that the ideas are no longer reality-based but abstract, and indeed substitute, notional concepts for reality. An example of such developments is seen in the terms used for the image of God. The more abstract our name for God, the less personal is our attachment to God – indeed here lies the danger of a purely theoretical, notional relationship to God. In such instances Fr Kentenich emphasizes the need for *fides caritate formata*. His names for God are the God of life, God of history, God of the Altar, God of my heart, God our Father, God of mercy and love.

Bridge between heaven and earth

Corresponding to the natural organism of attachments is the supernatural organism of attachments. Here in particular we look at the network of persons: the triune God, Mary, the saints and angels and the departed faithful. The place of the supernatural organism of attachments can be seen symbolically in the search for the paradise lost and the new home prepared for us by Christ. Evangelization starts there, where we form lasting bridges between these two networks. Kentenich describes the laws governing the growth of the relationship between heaven and earth: The relationship concerns itself with God and the world, and thus he calls them the world laws. The 'constitution' founding the relationship between God and his creation is described by Kentenich, following St Francis de Sales, as the law of love. God does everything out of love, for love and through love. Kentenich developed from this foundation a group of four laws, which form the central statements of his teaching on secondary causes. The four laws are (1) the law to govern the world; (2) the law governing the interaction and interplay of order in the different dimensions of the world; (3) the law to bring the world to perfection; and (4) the law of divine adaptation.[29]

The laws of God's governance

Kentenich sees normal human attachment as the way to attachment to God. Love is learned in most cases by our experience of loving parents, people I am otherwise attached to and places and things of our world. The right order is that metaphysically, theologically, God and our love of God come

first. Life's way to teach us this is that the natural attachments to all in the world eventually become more and more
symbols of our relationship to God, and they themselves are
seen in the context of being the secondary cause of our love
and attachment ultimately to God. This law has a key to
understanding the rules for effective evangelization through
the organism of attachments: *Deus operatur per causas secun-
das liberas* (God works through free secondary causes). This
law offers a framework (described above), which illustrates
the development of all natural bonds and their extended
growth to bonding with God. Love is learned in the context of
daily life. The growth of our attachments is part of the process
of development of the human person. Generally this law
describes our participation in qualities and characteristics
associated with the Creator: wisdom, goodness and power. A
person's gift of love, respect, trust and obedience to another
person (e.g., a child to its parent or members of a religious
community to their superior) can only be acceptable and
understood in so far as the intermediary becomes a symbol for
God. These elements of attachment belong in the end to God.
Created secondary causes as the subjects of this bond are
healthy in so far they lead us to our final goal in God. This
means that we can truly and in fact love God in loving our
neighbour, to the extent that this love becomes the symbol and
expression and guarantee of the greater, unseen dimension of
this love. Kentenich describes this (in psychological terms) as
the law of organic transference and transparence. Our
attachment to persons, places, things and ideas falls within
this framework, and these attachments are made transparent
in the underlying attachment to God.

The second law describes the relationship between the
higher order of the divine and the lower order of the created
world. There is a reciprocal relationship between the two
orders. The lower order is the 'expression, way and means and
guarantee' of the higher order. The love we express to our parents becomes an expression of our love for God. The love
of married couples is the expression of their love for God in
their love for one another. It is a concrete way and means of

realizing that love, and forms a guarantee for our deeper spiritual love. The higher order then shares its qualities with the lower order without the lower order losing its character. This means that the love between partners in marriage really shares in the quality of the divine, in so far as the love of the couple is a reflection of Christ's love for his Church. This love remains natural human love; however, it cannot possess absolute autonomy but falls into the framework of God's love for his creation. The third law describes the ascendance to God through attachment to the world being made transparent to the Creator. The fourth law describes God's adaptation to the limitations of our senses and perspectives.

The importance of a network of attachments, both natural and supernatural, for evangelization in the modern world is that the culturing of an organism of attachments, both naturally and supernaturally, enables us to form deep personal bonds anchored in the core of our being. These bonds allow transcendence from this world to God. Secondly, they enable sustainable growth, both in the faith and in the community.

Conclusion

Looking at the elements of classical evangelization, we see the complex of *kerygma*, *koinonia* and *diakonia*. To serve the purpose of evangelization, we see that the development of the organism of attachments means that the framework for the growth of truth in the Good News happens within the growth of personal emotional attachment to Christ through the support of a healthy organism of natural attachments. The strong emphasis in modern times on a communio-theology is served well through the development of the model of family and home found in the organism of attachments. Serving God's people and helping to build the kingdom finds renewable sources of energy in the network of strong attachments. The personalization of the task strengthens the motivation and awakens new sources of strength.

Notes

1. Philip Knights and Andrea Murray, *Evangelisation in England and Wales: A report to the Catholic Bishops* (London: Catholic Communications, 2002). (Hereafter referred to as *Evangelisation 2002*.)
2. Ibid., p. 75.
3. Ibid., pp. 75ff.
4. Ibid., p. 76.
5. See recent developments in politics and the effect on perceived ethics and morals (e.g., the Gender Recognition Bill under consideration which will allow persons of acquired gender to have their original documents of birth changed, this information then becoming information which cannot be disclosed under the Data Protection Act).
6. Cf. *Evangelisation 2002*, pp. 76ff.
7. See Letter to Diognetus, Chapters 5 and 6. (c. late 2nd century CE)

> For the Christians are distinguished from other men neither by country, nor language, nor the customs which they observe. For they neither inhabit cities of their own, nor employ a peculiar form of speech, nor lead a life which is marked out by any singularity. The course of conduct which they follow has not been devised by any speculation or deliberation of inquisitive men; nor do they, like some, proclaim themselves the advocates of any merely human doctrines. But, inhabiting Greek as well as barbarian cities, according as the lot of each of them has determined, and following the customs of the natives in respect to clothing, food, and the rest of their ordinary conduct, they display to us their wonderful and confessedly striking method of life. 18 They dwell in their own countries, but simply as sojourners. As citizens, they share in all things with others, and yet endure all things as if foreigners. Every foreign land is to them as their native country, and every land of their birth as a land of strangers. They marry, as do all [others]; they beget children; but they

do not destroy their offspring. 19 They have a common table, but not a common bed. 20 They are in the flesh, but they do not live after the flesh. 21 They pass their days on earth, but they are citizens of heaven. 22 They obey the prescribed laws, and at the same time surpass the laws by their lives. They love all men, and are persecuted by all. They are unknown and condemned; they are put to death, and restored to life. 23 They are poor, yet make many rich; 24 they are in lack of all things, and yet abound in all; they are dishonoured, and yet in their very dishonour are glorified. They are evil spoken of, and yet are justified; they are reviled, and bless; 25 they are insulted, and repay the insult with honour; they do good, yet are punished as evildoers. When punished, they rejoice as if quickened into life; they are assailed by the Jews as foreigners, and are persecuted by the Greeks; yet those who hate them are unable to assign any reason for their hatred. (Chapter 5, 'The Manners of the Christians')

To sum up all in one phrase – what the soul is to the body, so are Christians to the world. The soul is dispersed through all the members of the body, and Christians are scattered through all the cities of the world. The soul dwells in the body, yet is not of the body; and Christians dwell in the world, yet are not of the world. 26 The invisible soul is guarded by the visible body, and Christians are known indeed to be in the world, but their godliness remains invisible. (Chapter 6, 'The Relation of Christians to the World')

8. *Evangelii Nuntiandi*, 18–20.
9. Lee A. Kirkpatrick, 'Attachment and religious representations and behaviour', in J. Cassidy and P.R. Shaver (eds), *Handbook of Attachment: Theory, Research and Clinical Applications* (New York: Guilford, 1999), pp. 803–22.
10. Ibid., pp. 806ff.
11. The phenomenon of a change in mindset from mechanistic

to organic thinking is seen as the onset of a change in paradigm. Fritjof Capra says that organic thinking relieves us of an already bankrupt mechanistic image of the world. Quoted in Hubertus Brantzen *et al.* (eds), *Schönstatt Lexikon, Fakten Ideen Leben* (Vallender, Patris Verlag, 1996), p. 288.

12. Lothar Penners, *Eine Pädagogig des katholischen, Schönstatt-Studien 5* (Schönstatt: Patris Verlag, 1983), p. 256.

13. J. Kentenich, *Das Lebensgeheimnis Schönstatts*, Vol. 2 (Vallender: Patris Verlag, 1972), p. 149.

14. Penners, *Eine Pädagogig*, p. 279.

15. For Bowlby the principal attachment figures lie within the traditional family: mother, father, older siblings and perhaps grandparents. In a normal household the selected principal attachment figure is the tie to the mother-figure. John Bowlby, *Attachment and Loss*, Vol. I (London: Penguin, 1984), p. 305.

16. Cf. Günther M. Boll, 'Bindungspädogogik', in Brantzen *et al.* (eds), *Schönstatt Lexikon*, p. 31.

17. J. Kentenich, *Das Lebensgeheimnis Schönstatts*, Vol. 2, pp. 165ff. In the following passages concerning the dimensions of the organism of attachments to persons, places, created things and ideas see Brantzen *et al.* (eds), *Schönstatt Lexikon*, pp. 34ff.

18. A starting-point for the Church means creating space for families. The recent initiative of the Bishops' Conference of England and Wales seeks to address this issue (Listening 2004). The Church has to become a place where all families – in the fullest spectrum of the term – have to be made welcome. This should be achieved without the image of Catholic marriage and family life losing its 'beacon status'; as such the image of family becomes at the same time inclusive and challenging. Having a real yardstick to measure by brings security and deeper acceptance, especially when there is irregular circumstance. When we look down the line of those we wish to reach in the process of evangelization, we see that in each case the

establishment of personal relationships builds bridges to finding a way to the Church.

19. Kirkpatrick, 'Attachment and religious representations and behaviour', pp. 812ff.
20. Cf. Herta Schlosser in Brantzen *et al.* (eds), *Schönstatt Lexikon*, pp. 286–91.
21. Raymond E. Brown, *The Gospel according to John, The Anchor Bible*, Vol. 29 (New York, London, Toronto, Sydney Auckland: Doubleday, 1966), pp. 176ff.
22. J. Kentenich, *Dass neue Menschen werden: eine pädagogische Religionspsychologie* (Schönstatt: Patris Verlag, 1978), p. 127.
23. Pestalozzi, quoted in J. Kentenich, *Kindsein vor Gott, Priesterexerzitien* (Retreat for Priests held in 1937), ed. Günther M. Boll and Lothar Penners (Vallender: Patris Verlag, 1979), p. 73. See also J. Kentenich, *Dass neue Menschen werden*, p. 185.
24. Ibid., p. 186.
25. Christa Meves, *Erziehen lernen aus tiefenpsychologisher Sicht* (Munich: Bayerischer Schulbuch-Verlag, 1981), pp. 171ff.
26. Kentenich, *Dass neue Menschen werden*, pp. 176ff.
27. Cf. M.A. Nailis, *Werktagsheiligkeit* (Limburg: Lahn-Verlag, 1974), especially on 'Prophetische Dinggebundenheit'.
28. J. Kentenich, *Studie* (unpublished manuscript, 1949), p. 216.
29. Cf. Brantzen *et al.* (eds), *Schönstatt Lexikon*, pp. 426ff. See also, *Causa Secunda, Textbuch zur Zweitursachenlehre bei P. Josef Kentenich*, ed. J. Kentenich-Institut, (Freiburg: Causa Secunda, 1979), p. 10.

6

'I will Bless you, Father, Lord of Heaven and Earth, for Hiding these Things from the Learned and the Clever': The L'Arche Experience of Evangelization

Christine McGrievy

Our world is for those who are successful, who are rich, who are productive, who are strong; it is for those who are beautiful, those who are competitive, those who win. Our lives and ways of relating to our environment, and even with one another, are routinely based on materialism and consumerism. Many technical advances – in medicine, in communications and other areas – have changed our lives in a multitude of ways, often for the better. And yet something essential is lacking. Our world is full of tension, of stress; it is violent and people are afraid. Our relations with one another are so often based on fear, on mistrust, on competition . . . and the rich and strong get richer and stronger, while the poor and vulnerable become more and more vulnerable as the gap between them grows.

In the Christian tradition we understand that God, with unconditional love for our world, in the desire to bring us to life, sent his Son Jesus into this world. Jesus came to us in the total vulnerability of a newborn child. He was not born into a rich and powerful family but into the ordinariness of a family from Nazareth. His birth took place not even in the family home but in the messiness of an outbuilding in Bethlehem, surrounded not by adoring crowds but by lowly animals. In the first years of his life, Jesus, together with his family, suffered the fear and pain of exile. But he was born into a tradition of faith and nourished in the ancient Jewish conviction that God cares for the poor and dispossessed. A poor itinerant preacher and healer, he witnessed to the compassion of the Father and spoke prophetic words of hope to an oppressed people. He saw that the economy of God's reign is different from that of the world, and that in God's economy the poor possess riches of the spirit and a kind of wisdom that is easily missed by the wealthy and powerful. It was not a widely welcomed or even easily grasped message in his time – or today, for that matter. At the end of his life he suffered the pain of an ignominious death on a cross, surrounded by two brigands and mocking crowds.

The Beatitudes, preached by Jesus on a hillside in Galilee, profoundly summarize the ancient Judaeo-Christian conviction that God is especially with the poor and that in a mysterious way the poor are rich and carry gifts for the rest of us. This teaching has been a source of guidance and inspiration for L'Arche from its founding.

The place of people with developmental disabilities has evolved greatly over time. Government legislation in many countries has tried to improve their living conditions and advocacy groups around the world have forced societies to become ever more inclusive. And yet, we hear still of mistreatment in psychiatric hospitals. Recent reports from certain Eastern European countries come to mind. In places in Latin America and in Africa children and adults with development disabilities are locked up or tied up in their homes. But we in richer countries should not feel smug. In Australia a significant percentage of the prison population are people with development difficulties, and many are having to live on the streets, as an unwanted but direct consequence of de-institutionalization. In fact, in many of our own Western societies where de-institutionalization has been fairly successful, there are those who fall through the cracks and those who, while set up in independent apartments, live lonely lives.

In Europe and in North America abortions are on the increase and we hear more and more of our potential to produce 'designer babies', genetically 'engineered' to parents' specifications. In France a couple of years ago a survey showed that over 90 per cent of women who know that the child they are carrying has a handicap opt for an abortion. The situation of people with developmental disabilities remains one of fragility and vulnerability. For a child or a woman or man to have a developmental disability is often regarded as a scandal in human terms. It is hard to understand and hard to accept in our society. Sometimes seeing a disability is so hard to bear that we either deny the difference and want to ignore it, or we want to hide it away. Suffering and death, disfigurement and vulnerability are difficult realities to be in the presence of, in our modern Western world. Our culture lives on success and the values it engenders, and it cannot cope well with perceived failure.

In stunning contrast, the Gospel message takes us beyond the values of success and into the mystery of the lives of these people who are seen as so limited and whose very existence is seen as such an embarrassment, into the mystery of their giftedness and the presence of God within them. Through this message, and through opening ourselves to its embodiment in people who have a disability, perhaps we begin to discover the deep need we ourselves have, whole and rich in spirit as we may seem, for those who are weak and vulnerable. This is a need that is fundamental to our own personal human and spiritual journey, but it is also a need of our society, our world. In order for our society to be human, to be humane, we need those who are 'on the bottom of the pile', those who are poor, who are vulnerable ... people with developmental disabilities, the elderly, those in palliative care, those with nothing.

I can testify to this need in my own journey. Coming to L'Arche from university, I met Edith, a young lady with profound disabilities who had just arrived from the local psychiatric hospital. My desire, of course, was to be the 'good assistant', to be of help, and to be kind. Edith was in anguish, her pain palpable, and she deeply needed others to care for her. She was not capable of wearing a mask and was totally vulnerable, her need laid open and bare for all to see. In the face of Edith's stark reality, I began to discover my own shadow-side, my lack of patience, lack of acceptance, the protective walls within me, the capacity I could feel for violence when confronted by my own sense of powerlessness. In face of this anguish Edith offered me total acceptance of who I was, all my inadequacies included. For me she manifested the gift of forgiveness and helped me understand reconciliation in a deeper way. I was led to a new discovery of Jesus, of God and God's love for me, in my vulnerability. I came to see Edith and God and myself as being in a trinitarian relationship. Gradually I have come to recognize that this image of trinity can be at the base of all my relationships.

A few weeks ago I was in my community house celebrating Holy Thursday. Easter is one of the most important times of the year as we accompany Jesus in his last days, from the washing of his disciples' feet, through the Last Supper, the stations of the cross and Jesus's death on the cross, the long wait of Holy Saturday until the joy of the resurrection. On Holy Thursday, after having washed one another's feet we share with one another our history and God's faithfulness in all of the journey. As a L'Arche household we realized that in the 21 years of our existence we had welcomed almost 200 assistants to make a home with us, some for a few weeks, others for a year or two and some for four, five or six years or more. All of them had been transformed by their relationships with the people with learning disabilities and all had taken the gifts they had received to wherever they settled. They continue touching the lives of those they meet. My personal experience of growth and transformation, although unique to me, is shared by the many, many people who come into the lives of the people with learning difficulties in our communities, into relationship with Edith, Jean-Luc, Brian, Francie, Dieudonné and others.

I want to describe three fundamental aspects of this common experience of transformation through relationship with those who are poor:

The opening of the heart

Whether aware of it or not, we human beings are often filled with prejudices, closed up behind inner walls or barriers, and when we enter into relationships we frequently try to have power over others, who quickly become rivals. This dynamic occurs in our personal relationships but also amongst groups and between nations. People with developmental disabilities cry out for relationship, for affection, for faithful friendship and understanding, and they have a mysterious way of breaking down those barriers around our hearts and awakening what is deepest within all of us – our common humanity. Many young people arriving in our communities today come from broken family backgrounds, their lives based more on 'having' and 'doing' than on 'being with', and for many of them it is at first a struggle to enter into relationships where the 'being' is essential.

In this regard, Antonio comes to mind. Antonio was a severely disabled young man who had many limitations. He did not make a lot of noise, could not 'do' things, and yet was a great teacher and transformed the lives of young people who came to spend some time sharing his home. He brought people in touch with their heart. He called the assistants just to accept themselves and him, to a mutual listening to the almost silent language of love and compassion; to touch that is not merely functional but recognizes the humanity of the other, to just 'being with'. For the assistant such a relationship becomes a path to self-knowledge and inner healing and personal integration.

There are two forms of compassion. One manifests as competent and efficient action. Antonio, especially at the end of his life, needed the assistants to care for his body, which was covered with bedsores, and he needed massage to help him breathe more peacefully. But Antonio also needed the second type of compassion – the compassion that is to empathize with, to suffer with, the compassion where we accept just to be with Antonio, to share the littleness of his life, and to look and touch and speak with tenderness and love – to be present when there is nothing to be done.

The welcome of difference

One of the greatest difficulties for us today is to accept those
who are different. We all tend to look for people who think like
us, who have the same tastes, the same type of life-style. We
know the tensions around welcoming people from other countries into our own country and the challenges around ecumenism and interreligious dialogue for us in our churches. There
seems to be a pervading 'us and them' attitude in society, and
it can influence us in spite of our best intentions. It is evident
on the football pitches and it flows over into the streets and
into hooliganism. We recall it in the age-old 'love–hate' relationship between the French and the British. When we at
L'Arche come into our communities there seems to be an obvious divide: there are those who have a disability and those
who do not. In institutions this difference is seen as essential,
and the divide is never to be crossed. People who work in such
places talk about 'professional distance' in their relationships
and pride themselves in maintaining this. And yet, unless we
take the risk of letting down our barriers and allowing a meeting of hearts we lose something of the gift that is to be received
from the other, and also we lose an essential part of who we
are ourselves.

Moses is a young boy who was abandoned by his mother and
found on the streets in Zimbabwe. He was welcomed into one
of our communities. Rejected by his own family, he was unable
to look after himself and was very dependent, and yet he was
not afraid of the other, of being in relationship. Moses' heart is
open to welcome and to love, and he opens up the hearts of
those who come into contact with him. As Moses and others
like him touch the hearts of those who come to share the home,
these assistants are called into that same type of welcome: a
welcome which comes out of an acceptance of the other and
their vulnerability.

As assistants, our hearts are transformed in these relationships. As we become less afraid of the vulnerability of Moses,
of Antonio, we can begin to touch our own vulnerability and be
a little less afraid there also. Moses and Antonio help us touch
that shadow part of us, the part that we want to hide or to

deny, our violence, our desire for power, for domination; and yet they also take us into our own yearning to be accepted, to be loved for who we are. We discover that we are all part of one humanity, that we are all part of God's creation, that we are all first and foremost daughters and sons of God. And if we share a common humanity, those of us who have a so-called disability and those of us who (officially) do not, then we must also share this common humanity with those who are not of the same Church tradition, or religion or race.

In September 2001, one of the people with learning disabilities in my community died. Thierry had not had an easy life. He suffered a great deal of anguish and yet in his peculiar way had touched the hearts of many people over the almost 30 years that he spent with us. He had been unwell for some time and so that summer stayed with a group in the community for the holidays, with Nadia a young Moroccan, a Muslim, who had come to help. During the holidays, things went surprisingly well for Thierry and yet the very first day back to normal routine he was rushed to hospital and died. It was a hard time for everyone in the community, but we were able to give support to one another and find strength and hope through prayer. One important time was just after a eucharist when some of us went to the room where Thierry's body was lying, to pray again with him, and there we found Nadia, singing her prayers to accompany Thierry in his final passage. For us to be there as she sang was a deeply prayerful experience of communion in suffering and in hope, of being part of God's family.

Ten days later, came the frightening events of 9/11. Nadia was an assistant in my house, along with a young Serb, a German, a man from Quebec and myself. We were living with six people with developmental disabilities, one of whom was also a Muslim. Again, it was so important for us to share the pain together and to choose to be open with one another, to trust and to be vulnerable. It was obvious that the choice we were making was not just for ourselves, not just on an 'affective' level, an emotional level, but that it was a choice to recognize and espouse being of one family, of God's family, choosing to be sisters and brothers, choosing for a common humanity. And in a way it was a choice for hope for our world.

In Isaiah 49.6, the prophet refers to the messianic mission: 'It is not enough for you to be my servant, to restore the tribes of Jacob and bring back the survivors of Israel; I shall make you a light to the nations so that my salvation shall reach the remotest parts of earth.' Whether we understand these words as the Jewish people do, as a promise for the future for which we are invited to help prepare the ground through acts that mend our world, or whether we understand them as Christians, as a call for us to complete the work of Jesus our Messiah, the message of hope for unity is the same.

In the federation today we have 124 communities in 30 different countries; they are places of welcome for all those who want to share our lives, and so bring together people of differing intellectual capacity, social origin, religion and culture. In fact they represent only a very small number of people – a drop in the ocean. And yet I firmly believe that every gesture, every word which crosses the divide of difference, is a step towards the breaking down of barriers in our world, the uniting of the human family and the building of God's kingdom. God, who is the source of all being, of all creation, has placed us in a world of diversity and invites us to meet him in that diversity, to find him in the face of the one who is different.

Forgiveness and reconciliation

As we share our lives more and more deeply with those who are different, we discover our own limitations, our own prejudices and our own lack of freedom. We discover our need to control situations and people, and our own anger and propensity for conflict.

Attractive as it often seems to outsiders, life in our communities is not just one long picnic. Living with those who have gone through a great deal of pain and who experience times of distress and anguish, living with those who come from different family backgrounds, and from different educational, religious and cultural backgrounds leads to tensions and hurt, suffering and pain. These are part of our daily lives. For this reason, community life would be impossible without forgiveness.

I have lived with Michèle for over 25 years. Michèle's capacity to bring assistants to the end of their tether is widely acknowledged among those who have lived with her. Being with Michèle has helped me understand mothers who react aggressively when faced with their own incapacity to lessen the pain and anguish of their child. Yet Michèle has an amazing capacity to forgive. Forgiveness for Michèle is to stay in relationship, to continue to trust, to continue to accept that we give her care in the very personal ways she needs.

When I think of Michèle, and when I think of the challenges of living with such a diverse group of people, I am reminded of Jesus's teaching: 'Be compassionate as your Father is compassionate. Do not judge and you will not be judged. Do not condemn and you will not be condemned. Forgive and you will be forgiven. Give and it will be given to you' (Lk. 6.36–8).

L'Arche is first and foremost a place where we discover our own humanity: a place where we discover what it is to be human. In L'Arche and wherever there is a true meeting with those who are vulnerable, people discover that to be human – and to be Christian – means to love people. Things and projects are important, but should always be orientated towards people; the road to conflict-resolution and justice can only come through dialogue, relationship and love. Assistants come to do good and then discover that the people with learning disabilities heal them and transform them, leading them into compassion. They often come motivated by generosity, they want to 'give' to those who 'have' less, and then, as they enter into relationships with the people with developmental disabilities, they discover a mutuality – we are in need of one another. The person who is vulnerable needs the competencies and capacities of the 'assistant' in order to live well and to develop, while we assistants need the person with developmental disabilities to help us recognize our own need for loving relationships and to help us enter into a greater knowledge and acceptance of who we are, with our inner light and our shadows and our vulnerability, and thereby to enter into a greater wholeness of being.

When this happens, the community becomes a place where everyone is needed, every member is a leader at the point of her gift, and every member is a follower at the point of the gift of the other person. No one can be excluded. To exclude would make us incomplete, as St Paul reminds us in his letter to the Corinthians:

> As it is, God has put all the separate parts into the body as he chose. If they were all the same part, how could it be a body? As it is, the parts are many but the body is one . . . What is more, it is precisely the parts of the body that seem to be the weakest which are the indispensable ones. It is the parts of the body which we consider least dignified that we surround with the greatest dignity . . . God has composed the body so that greater dignity is given to the parts which were without it . . .' (1 Cor. 12.18–24)

This same truth applies to the wider world. There is a need for the intelligent, the wise and the strong, but in order for a society to be human and welcoming for all, there needs to be a solidarity with those who are seen as weak and vulnerable. The disabled, the weak, have the gift of opening up the hearts of the intelligent; they help us recognize our own poverty and disabilities and so open the eyes of the 'wise' to new and essential truths about what it is to be human. They show us, 'the strong', that we cannot control everything, that there is a limit to our power, and that when we misuse that power it can result in violence.

The gift of the poor person thus leads toward unity. As Paul continues, we give greater honour (or a 'preferential option', as the Roman Catholic Church puts it) to the poor, 'so that there may not be disagreements inside the body but each part may be equally concerned for all the others. If one part is hurt, all the parts share its pain. And if one part is honoured, all the parts share its joy' (1 Cor. 12.25–26).

L'Arche is about entering into relationships, entering with a humility and desire for truth which allow ourselves to be transformed by those relationships. It is those relationships and their fruits – love, freedom, joy and wholeness – which are a sign and a gift for our world.

L'Arche is about the 'power' of the 'powerless' – their capacity to open hearts, to help the rest of us to become more fully human, to evangelize us, if you will. In L'Arche, we do not seek to proselytize. Indeed, our charter commits us to support each person in their own faith. But what we have discovered is that the relationship with the person with a disability contains in it the good news that we are profoundly accepted, loved and forgiven, just as we are. Thus it can be an avenue for spiritual growth. Assistants who come without a faith, or with a very nominal Christian experience, often find that their time at L'Arche opens up a path to faith. In the teachings of Jesus, they find words to put to their experience. For those who come to L'Arche as Christians, their relationships in L'Arche lead into a new and deeper experience of the mystery of the Gospel and to a more profound meeting with Jesus, and so with the Father and Creator of all.

7

Christian Initiation and the Transmission of Faith

Kiko Argüello

Let me start by introducing myself: I am Spanish and a painter by trade. I won a national prize for painting in Spain. I studied Fine Arts at the University of Madrid. At a certain point I left painting and went to live among the poor. I have been 20 years without painting, but now the Lord wants me to paint again. At this moment [March 2004] I am painting the Cathedral in Madrid. The Gospel is accomplished: 'He who leaves father, mother, his work will receive a hundredfold.' A hundredfold for me was to paint a huge Gothic cathedral, the whole of the apse of the cathedral, helped by a group of artists. Since I am a painter, I speak with brush-strokes: one here, one there, and I hope that the Holy Spirit will make you see a beautiful painting, because more important than painting a cathedral is to paint the face of Christ in your soul.

Europe is going through a very difficult time. It is really apostatizing from Christianity. Society has completely changed. In Spain, for instance, there has been massive immigration: people from Ecuador, from Morocco, and every day more people arrive.

To understand what is happening, think that today in France 50 per cent of people are unbaptized, and more than this, only 30 per cent of mothers bring their children to the parish for catechism. Out of 100 children, 70 have no relationship with the Church. The whole of society is changing in its attitude to issues such as: homosexuality, lesbianism, euthanasia, abortion, etc. Heterologous artificial insemination is now legal in Spain. It is terrible that these children will never know who their father is. This hurts the people and is unjust, because any young person wants to know who their father is. Even in Sweden heterologous insemination is forbidden, because they realize that most problems behind juvenile delinquency are linked with a missing father-figure in the family. We are moving towards a very harsh society, where 70 per cent of the people are single and living alone; there are thousands of women alone and in some places up to 60 per cent of these single women are alcoholics. The youth are abandoned to themselves. In Spain, thousands spend their weekends in the streets, drinking and taking drugs. The situation is so bad that the government has had to forbid drinking in the open.

Spain has the highest number of abortions among minors in Europe. We are moving towards a new, a different society, and what is most under threat in it is the family. It seems as if a demon has come out from the abyss, as the Apocalypse says, wanting to destroy the Christian family. Because, if it destroys the family, all of society will change. In Spain every four minutes a family breaks up. In the United States, in the past only young families broke up, but now even elderly couples are divorcing. They are splitting up after 40 or 50 years of marriage, and they don't know why. It is like a fashion, and everyone has to do it. Therefore many elderly people are alone. Society is becoming especially harsh towards the elderly. The homes for elderly people can be horrible.

A little anecdote. A nurse from the Neocatechumenal Way who works in one of these homes was telling us about it. It is a very rich home. There is a little hall with lights and a television, and all the elderly sit there. All of them constantly look over their shoulders, as with a nervous tic. She wondered what was happening. Eventually she realized that they were looking at the door, to see if someone from the family was coming in. It was not simply moving to see that, it was terrible. Years and years without anyone visiting them! Abandoned there to die. And their children and relatives think that they are doing the right thing, and that these elderly people are all very well.

I could go on, but I would like to stop and say that the Holy Spirit knew very well that the world was going to change: Internet, mobile phones, the media ... all is going faster and faster, the world is becoming smaller. McLuhan, a Canadian media expert who is a Catholic, a man with a prophetic vision of what the media culture would be, said that the world would become a global village, because in the future we would be able to know everything about everybody. If there is a bomb in South Africa, ten minutes later the whole world knows about it. We are entering into a new way of living, a new world; we are going towards a single culture, a 'monoculture'.

I say this because the Holy Spirit knew what was going to happen and prepared the Church with a Council. The Second Vatican Council started to prepare the Church for a new way of being a Church. The Council said something amazing. One of the constitutions of the Council is called *Lumen Gentium*, 'the Light of the Nations'. We are leaving behind 'Christendom', a situation where the whole society is Christian and all the schools are Christian. We are entering a world which will no longer be Christian: universities will not be Christian, schools will not be Christian, society will no longer be Christian and the television will be constantly preaching against revelation. The Church cannot continue any longer as it is, because it will become empty. In Copenhagen, the Lutherans have been selling their churches: five have been turned into brothels – luxury brothels. In Germany next year they will sell 1,000 Catholic churches!

It seems that things are very bad. But no, on the contrary: we are entering into a new time. I will give you another example, this time about Holland. Holland is interesting as it used to be devoutly Catholic. The Dutch are a very strong and daring people. When they received the Second Vatican Council they thought they had to implement it immediately and they started renewing churches, putting parishes in the hands of lay people. They came to think that to follow the Council meant to abandon Rome. What followed was a terrible decomposition in the Church. If you go to Holland now, you can see of all sorts of things happening in the parishes: theatre during Mass, or women going up to the altar with the chasuble to say Mass. They are opposing the bishops and all the hierarchy, especially Rome and the Pope, and they think they have implemented the Council. A whole part of the Church has totally misinterpreted the Council. This has resulted in polarization, because the other part, seeing the abuses, rejected the Council. They closed themselves to the renewal and went on with everything as it was before the Council: with the rails, with everybody kneeling, the cassocks, etc. If you go to Holland you will find these two polarities. God wants the Neocatechumenal Way to work with both. There is a *Redemptoris Mater* seminary in Amsterdam. It is a seminary coming from the Neocatechumenal Way, a missionary seminary for the whole world. The bishop appointed as parish priest a priest from that seminary. He has to confront these groups who are contesting the Church. It is very difficult, but we are announcing Jesus Christ to them. On the other hand, two years ago, the bishop of the diocese of Roermond near Maastricht, from the conservative wing of the Dutch Church, came to speak to us. 'I too want to open a *Redemptoris Mater* seminary,' he said. I told him that in order to open a seminary he needed to have the Neocatechumenal Way in his diocese, and he asked me, 'How do I open the Way in my diocese?' I said, 'I will send you a team: a couple, a priest and a lay person. You should gather the priests and explain to them what the Neocatechumenal Way is, hoping that some of the parish priests will agree to open it in their parishes.' Forty parish priests came to the meeting and ten of them decided to start, and catecheses were given in ten parishes at the same time. The Episcopal Vicar, who did not know anything about the Way, told us: 'You are the last chance for this diocese. If we fail with you we will pack up and close the churches, because here no one is coming anymore.' And this is a diocese where all the parishes are very traditional, the Masses seem Tridentine, everything looks as before the Council. They had thought that if they kept the Church as it traditionally was, people would come. In fact, the contrary happened.

Society is so aggressive, so violent, the catechesis against the Gospel is so continuous that no one goes to Church any longer. I say this to show you how important it is to implement the Council. On one hand the neoliberals have decomposed the parishes. They have not brought the Council, they have deformed it instead. The opposite sector refused to implement the Council, and no one is practising anymore.

I am speaking of the Council so that we may understand what the Neocatechumenal Way is. We are one of the new realities bringing the Council to the parishes. To implement the Council is a matter of life and death for the Church. How are we doing it? After the Council of Trent it would have been impossible to implement the Council if God had not raised up some new ecclesial realities: saints, charisms like the Jesuits' and many others: saints who for a century or more went about implementing the Council of Trent. Today we are one of the new realities bringing the Second Vatican Council to the parishes. We are very privileged: thanks to the Council we have a word for the postmodern man. Islam does not have this. The problem Islam has is that it realizes that society has changed and is extremely powerful, and feels threatened by it; its religiosity is threatened by modern society. In the Catholic Church, postmodernity, to give it a name, has brought about secularization and people have left the Church. All round us there are different sorts of people. How do we preach the Gospel in a society where people have been married three or four times and are now alone? Where women may have had many abortions and have problems with alcohol? It is precisely for these people that God has prepared the Neocatechumenal Way. What are we doing? I tell you what I told the 40 parish priests in Roermond. I said it is imperative that a Catholic parish should pass from pastoral work limited to administering the sacraments to pastoral work of evangelization.

Many people, because of secularization, no longer practise their faith, and in some parishes there is only a small group that continues to go to church. In one church 5 per cent of the parish population may go to Mass, in another 10 per cent, in another 1 per cent and in another 20 per cent. Only a small group is still practising. They go to church, they bring the children to catechism, they marry in the church. The parish priest tries to carry out pastoral work based on the sacraments, to bring people to Christ. Where is Christ? Christ is present in the sacraments, in the bishops, the priests, etc. . . .

he is present in the eucharist, baptism, confession and all the other sacraments. He is present in the poor and the suffering. This parish priest, if Christ is present in the Mass, has to celebrate Mass. He has to prepare people for baptism. If Christ is present in the sacrament of marriage, he has to prepare people for marriage, if Christ is present in the poor, the priest has to organize all the charity. This is a pastoral work. But there is a problem: all that the priest is doing in the parish is of no use for those who no longer go to church. And why do they not go? Well, to believe that Christ is in the eucharist you need faith. To believe that Christ is in marriage you need faith. To believe that Christ is present in the bishop you need more faith. And these people no longer have faith.

All this pastoral work at the most will keep in touch with the people who have already got faith. But it is not missionary, it has no possibility of evangelizing, and when the Church is no longer missionary it is no longer the Church of Christ, because the essence of the Church is being missionary. God has given himself to the Church, and he is the truth. Then, in order to reach the person outside – maybe your sister who left the Church, who is living with a partner and has stopped coming to church, or your cousin, or your aunt: people who were baptized and have left the Church – to reach this person, in order for her to come back to the Church, we need to find a presence of Jesus Christ that does not presuppose faith. The question is: does this presence exist? Does such a presence of Christ exist, that when one sees it he is drawn to him? Yes, it exists. Let us see what is written in the Gospel. Our Lord Jesus Christ says: 'Love one another as I have loved you. By this love that man will know you are my disciples. If you are perfectly one, that man will believe.' That man who today has no faith, if he sees love among us, he will believe. Christ said: 'as I have loved you'. Christ loved us; how did Christ love us? Christ loved us so much that he died for us. Christ loved us this way, and he tells us to love each other this way.

Have you seen a Christian loving this way? The Council has spoken of the Church as a sacrament of salvation. A sacrament is something that you can see, it is a sign, and the

Church is a sign. When someone sees a Union Jack it reminds him of England. If this sister here reached the point of loving like that, if she loves like this, her faith becomes a sign, becomes a sacrament, becomes light, light of the nations, *Lumen Gentium*. The issue is not that there should be many Christians, but that the light may appear.

Christ was crucified for us. This means that he has taken our sins upon himself. To have this sort of love means that the Christians allow themselves to be crucified. It means to take upon oneself the sins of others. Have you seen this? Can you say: 'That person is a Christian, I have seen him going on the cross!' When someone sees this he will say: 'I've never met anybody like that; I've never seen such a thing anywhere.' Then he would draw closer and see the light. This crucified man here, Christ, is God. Christians receive from heaven the Holy Spirit, who gives us the very nature of God and makes us love this way.

What is the Neocatechumenal Way doing? We go to a parish and we say: 'In order to reach all these people we need to form a community where people love each other as Christ loved us on the cross. To reach that stature in the faith we need to implement a Christian initiation.' How can we reach that dimension of faith? (People have very little faith.) How can we make that faith grow in us? By following an itinerary of Christian initiation where we go through all the stages of baptism.

In the Early Church, baptism was represented by seven steps going down to a pool of water. We have to go down this way, descending these steps. Living in a Christian community, we will start to realize how difficult it is for us to love our neighbour when he is different from us. We are unable to love 'the other' when the other kills us. We are unable to allow ourselves to be killed. We cannot love beyond death, because we are dead inside, because there is sin in us and sin causes our interior man to die. How many dead people are there in London? Many. For this reason they split, they divorce. The Church explains what sin is: man who makes himself God. How many of you, here, are constantly doing your own will in your lives? You are directing your own lives. An ancient

Father said: 'What is the science of the saints? Humility? No. Obedience? No. Asceticism? No. What is the science of the saints? To do the will of God, because Christians no longer live in themselves.' In baptism Christians are submerged in the waters of Christ's death. When they come out, they are a new creation; they are no longer living for themselves, they live in Christ. St Paul says: 'It is no longer I who live, it is Christ who lives in me.' How many Christians are here today? This is an interesting question. How many here are not living for themselves, Christ is living in them instead, and they are always doing the will of God? To them, living is Christ; they are Christ, the body of Christ. And Christ is God. 'Anyone who listens to you listens to me; anyone who rejects you rejects me; and those who reject me reject the one who sent me' (Lk. 10.16). This is Christianity.

We are leading people through the different stages of baptism, so that the old man in them may die to himself, to his own ego; they are buried in baptism, so that they may be reborn to a new life, forming a Christian community. This is the process of Christian initiation. When a community has been formed, after a number of years they choose some catechists to give catechesis to form another community, and then another and another one, and the parish is transformed into a community of communities – a sort of 'atomic' structure. In Rome there are parishes with 30 communities, others with 25, 20, 18 communities, all full of young people. In Rome there are 111 parishes with a total of 600 communities; in Madrid 67 parishes.

The parish of Canadian Martyrs in the centre of Rome has 30 communities. You know that parishes in the centre of big cities are empty; they die because young people move to the suburbs. The parish priest was saying that no one was coming any longer, and I told him: 'If in this parish a small Christian community is formed, a community of 40 or 50 brothers, and they follow an itinerary, in obedience to their catechists (because without obedience there is no growing in faith), one day you will not know where to fit all the people who come to your church.' Today there are 30 communities and there is literally no room for all these people. They recently started a new catechesis and they had 200 people coming, many of them divorced, separated, lots of homosexuals, lesbians – all the normal people of the world. They come because they have seen Christ crucified in the person working with them, or in a relative. Light of the nations! Outside this church on a Saturday evening there are 400 young people waiting to attend the eucharist in different communities. It is a spectacle, something to be seen. Why are these young people coming to church instead of going dancing? They are 18 and if their parents tried to make them go to Mass in the community it would be useless: they are free, they are over 18, they do not have to go; but they want to go.

I don't know if you realize what I'm talking about. A very serious sociological change is taking place everywhere in the world. In front of this change, the Council – through us as well as through others – is bringing about another change: a passage from pastoral work based on the temple to pastoral work based on the Christian community. This means going back to the pastoral work of the Acts of the Apostles. I tell you that in a few years' time no one in the Church will think it is possible for a priest to survive alone, without his own community. To live our faith in a community is something fantastic; in the community there is that sister who has received from God the gift of being humble, or this young person who has received the gift of being brave, and with his courage he is helping me in my faith. There is a couple who are marvellous . . . Can you see the riches of the charisms in a Christian community? Do you understand? To live faith in a community is something wonderful, and this is our work. Our Lady told us: 'You must build Christian communities as the Holy Family of Nazareth, because in the Holy Family of Nazareth Christ became an adult.' Only as an adult could he fulfil his mission. So he lived for 30 years obeying Joseph and Mary. In all the Neocatechumenal communities there is this obedience to the catechists, and obedience helps faith to grow, slowly. We are not in a hurry. Even if many people don't understand us, and we face problems and many persecutions – it is a grace for a Christian

to be persecuted, his only medal is to resemble Christ crucified; if they insult you, if they slander you, it is a grace; if they
don't understand you . . . and sometimes the enemies are your
own children, your husband, your cousin – it doesn't matter.
Christians who are living in Christ save the world, because
they are carrying in their body what is lacking in the passion
of Christ.

I give you an example. From time to time we sent out a
number of brothers without money, as Christ sent the apostles
to announce the Gospel. One year we sent to Amsterdam a
Catholic priest and a layman from Australia, an Anglican who
had entered the Neocatechumenate. They were chosen at ran-
dom to go to Amsterdam, with the mission of visiting the parishes announcing Christ: that Christ has overcome death for
us and gives us eternal life. We sent them with the mission of
taking upon themselves the rejection, offering it for those who
were rejecting them. They had to do this mission without any
money. They arrived in Amsterdam with nothing, walking,
praying the rosary, with a cross and the Bible. They would
walk until they reached a parish. They met many priests, but
no one welcomed them and they spent several days without
eating anything and sleeping in the streets, in the cold. They
went to the railway station and at midnight they were thrown
out. After two days walking, without eating, they were in
pieces. They went to a parish and told the parish priest: 'The
peace of the Lord be with you! Christ loves you!' After announcing the *kerygma* they asked him: 'Could you give us something to eat? It's been two days since we last ate something.'
The priest told them: 'I will not give you anything, because
that crazy person who sent you has to learn that in this day
and age you cannot do these things.' And he gave them nothing. They left and carried on like this for five more days. No
one gave them anything and at the end their feet were bleed-
ing and they were dehydrated, but they were offering all this
for Amsterdam. Thanks to the suffering of these two people,
today in Amsterdam there are parishes with the Way, missionary families, a Redemptoris Mater seminary . . . Before,
there was nothing. This is the power of salvation that a

Christian has in Christ. This is true also here in England. If this brother is a Christian and at work they attack him and they slander him, he knows that through him God wants his son Jesus Christ to bring salvation to England. Not by preaching, but by being crucified. This is the tradition of the Church.

Christ loves us: how can we not love Christ? The Fathers of the desert say: Listen, my child, the love for Christ is the only truth. All the rest is vanity. Old age doesn't prevent you from loving Christ. Illness doesn't prevent you from loving Christ, poverty doesn't. We have been created to love God, and Christ is God. How many of you love Christ? Listen to St Paul: 'The one who does not love Christ is anathema', is cursed. Christ gave his life for you, for me. He has saved us from Hell. Christians no longer need to die; to die is to go with Christ who has overcome death for us. The Church announces wonderful news: Christ is risen! He has overcome death! Christians do not die; everyone else dies, Christians don't. They are part of the risen Christ. We don't know this as an illusion or an assent to some intellectual truth: we know this through faith. This is a supernatural gift; it is the greatest thing man can have. What is faith? Faith is the Spirit of Christ bearing witness to your spirit that God exists, that he loves you so much as to give his Son for you. Have you got this witness in you? Or, do you realize that you have no faith, that you never had faith? That is an important discovery, because then you will go and look for faith. Where can you find faith? Scripture says that faith comes through preaching. St Paul says: 'God wanted to save the world through the foolishness of preaching.' But if you go and check the Greek it does not say preaching, it says *kerygma*, an announcement of very important news. I can give this girl good news: God knows her problems, her suffering, her sins, he has sent his Son to give his life for her – and he died for her, so that she can receive from heaven a new life, eternal life: divine life dwelling in her.

There is something very important about divine nature; the letter to the Hebrews says: 'Christ is the exact imprint of the divine substance, imprinted in us. No one has ever seen

God.' This man on the cross is the exact imprint of the divine substance. What is this divine substance? It is love for you, total love, even if you are wicked, even if you are a murderer, a paedophile, a pervert, someone who destroys the work of God. Even if as soon as you see God you try to kill him, he loves you – and if you are a murderer he will accept being killed. Christ has really suffered death for you. Does God exist now? Where is God? If what I am saying is true, it means that the divine substance is love for you: God desires to be in you, to dwell in you. The Apocalypse says: 'I am at the door and I'm knocking.' You should open. 'If one opens my Father and I will enter in.' If you really love a woman, you want to be one with her. The love between a man and a woman is a reflection of the love of Christ for man. So, the divine substance wants to be in man. God has created you for this. But how can he enter, since he has made you free? The only way he has is to send me and, through the stupidity of my preaching, tell you: 'Believe in the good news, God wants to enter in you, he wants to love you. Leave sin, don't be afraid.' You may listen or not listen. Where this *kerygma* is announced, God is preparing a people to go to the world proclaiming the Gospel. God saved the world through the foolishness of the *kerygma*. While I speak of this to you, God is trembling, because he is waiting that someone among you may open himself up and believe that his life may change – not by his efforts, because Christianity is not based on our effort, but by the grace of God who sends us from heaven the Holy Spirit – and immediately this man who was maybe unable to forgive his wife, because he thought that she was really wrong, receives the grace of the Holy Spirit and finds out that, through the merits of Christ, through the gift of grace, he is able to forgive her and they won't separate. For this, in the Neocatechumenal Way, couples are not splitting; it is a work of the Holy Spirit in them which allows them to forgive each other. It is not a question of being good or bad: the fact is that God gives them his Spirit.

Christian communities save the family. In the Neocatechu-menal communities there are thousands of families, with many children. We say that the Christian family has three altars. The first altar is the altar of the eucharist; the second is the nuptial bed where the spouses give life to children. Christian families live the conjugal act as something sacred; they pray to God because they know that in making love they are celebrating a sacrament. Sexuality in Christianity is something marvellous. The problem is that no one has ever educated you to live your sexuality in a Christian way. Today we are witnessing the destruction of sexuality as God made it for man.

The third altar is the table, where the family gathers together to eat, because food comes from God who made marvellous things like potatoes and cabbages. Around that same table you pass the faith to your children. We have understood how necessary it is to have a domestic liturgy in the family: a domestic celebration, where parents can transmit and hand over the faith to their children. God appeared on Mount Sinai after having taken the Hebrews out of slavery from Egypt and having opened the sea. When God brings them to the desert suddenly Mount Sinai is covered with fire and clouds. They hear the voice of God, who comes down to speak to his people. He says: '*Shema Israel*: listen Israel. I am the only one.' And then he says: 'You shall love me, God, with all your heart, with all your mind – that is your intelligence – and with all your strength' (and that means your money). And he continues: 'This Love you will pass on to your children.' The first of the Commandments is this – before the Ten Commandments there is this Word of God: 'You will teach this to your children, before they go to bed, when they get up in the morning, before they go out and play, you will tell your child what I have done with you: How you were slaves in Egypt, how I intervened . . .' You need to bear witness to your children. Too many Catholic families have delegated this task to the parish, but in an itinerary of Christian initiation, it is very important that families, on Sunday, have a domestic liturgy.

The domestic liturgy is very simple. After singing the psalms, which all the family joins in, with guitars, etc., a text is chosen, usually from the old Testament. After it has been read the father asks: 'What is this text telling you?' We explain that the word of God is always perfect and alive, and is speaking to us.

We are convinced that it is through Christian families, with their many children, that Europe will be saved.

8

The Lay Faithful and Christian Life

Luis Fernando Figari

1. The layperson

Reflection on the laity is a vital enterprise, especially if it is seen in relation to the mission of the Church. For us all to reflect on the mission of the layperson is to deepen one's own Christian life, the new Evangelization in which we all are called to work, and the construction of a more just and reconciled world.

Confusion and clarity

In spite of much writing and speaking on the subject, the question of who or what constitutes a layperson seems not to be fully understood yet.

To clarify our ideas we must look to the teachings of the Second Vatican Council. If we look carefully, we discover a wonderful panorama about the identity, mission and spirituality of the lay faithful. One cannot doubt that the Council fathers, guided by the Holy Spirit, have splendidly deepened in their own understanding of the mission of the laity in the Church and in the world.

It is also necessary to highlight the homogeneous development of the teachings of the Magisterium. It is worth noticing the light shone on the ecclesiastical identity of the laypersons in the reflections of successive synods of bishops, as well as in the general conferences of bishops in Latin America, where almost half of the world's Catholics live.

So much has been said and clarified. One might think that everything has been covered and that it just remains to put the teachings into practice. Maybe that is the main issue: action now! Yet, I believe that a consciousness of the lay identity has to be internalized in one's life, before active commitment. Maybe it is due to the lack of a clear conceptualization and personal internalization that we can find one of the main clues to explain the passivity of laity in the mission of the Church. For action should follow the process of internalizing faith.

The Council fathers taught: 'The Christian vocation by its very nature is also a vocation to the apostolate.'[1] Have we seen a general lay commitment to the apostolate? There are wonderful exceptions, of course, among them the ecclesial movements. However, the question in its general sense stands. Notwithstanding other causes such as subjectivism, functional agnosticism, secularism, etc., or even taking them into account, we would certainly see a very different world if lay Catholics understood their commitment to the apostolate.

However, it should be understood that following Jesus cannot be restricted to the apostolate. John Paul II said:

> Faith is often confined to episodes and fragments of life. Certain relativism tends to feed discriminating attitudes toward the content of Catholic doctrine and morals, accepted or rejected on the basis of subjective and arbitrary preference. So the faith received ceases to be lived as a divine gift, as an extraordinary opportunity for human and Christian growth, as a meaningful event, as conversion of life. Only a faith that sinks its roots in the Church's sacramental life, whose thirst is quenched at the sources of God's Word and Tradition, that becomes new life and a renewed understanding of reality, can make the baptized effectively capable of withstanding the impact of the prevailing secularized culture.[2]

If we look at history, we can say that the fact that there are non-practising Catholics is nothing new. In this context practice is understood as the commitment expected of a son or daughter of the Church, not including supererogatory activities which some faithful practise. The actual phenomenon is referred to the great numbers of non-practising baptized members of the Church.

In our time, Catholic identity in many is undermined and

replaced by a vague selection of usually self-chosen, Christian values and beliefs. People do not formally fall away from the Church, but in their practice and daily life they do. Faith and life become divorced. This is one of the most serious disorders that afflicts the people of God today.

However, we should also speak of the active lay faithful. Here too we find a lack of identity, which could be called lack of consciousness. This results in a notorious weakening of the laity. Latin American bishops have said that these people's lives 'reveal an inconsistency between the faith they claim to profess and practise, on the one hand, and the real-life involvement they assume in society on the other'.[3] The rupture in Christian life is expressed in the four fundamental rifts: 'of man with God, with self, with the brethren and with the whole of creation'.[4] Laity is particularly fragile in relation to these four deep clefts or ruptures, especially because of the insertion of laypersons in the world. Anyway, the lack of identity and coherence is expressed in lack of unity in personal life and apostolic commitment.

How else can we explain the phenomenon of 'the de-Christianization of countries with ancient Christian traditions'?[5] Since the communion ecclesiology of the Second Vatican Council implies quite clearly that each member of the Church has a mission in working so all humankind will enter into a relationship with Jesus, it is obvious that each one is also to be concerned with those peers in danger of losing their faith. So the 'de-Christianized' reality of many countries that used to have a Catholic identity is a clear sign of what is called active omission on the part of numerous laypersons. We could analyse how this responsibility extends to members of the hierarchy, but that would lead us away from our main concern in this chapter.

On the other hand, how else can we explain what I venture to call a 'new' distinction between quantitative and qualitative secularism – the former indicating the number of people who declare themselves Catholics or comply with the precept to support the Church[6] and the latter referring to practising Catholics? If we applied this measure of *qualitative secularism* to those brothers and sisters alluded to by John Paul II in *Ecclesia in Europa*, the numbers of people affected by qualitative secularism would rise accordingly. The Pope says: 'Many of the baptized live as if Christ did not exist: the gestures and signs of faith are repeated, especially in devotional practices, but they fail to correspond to a real acceptance of the content of the faith and fidelity to the person of Jesus.[7]

As we are in England, it is perhaps appropriate to look to Cardinal Newman for insight into the concept of lay men and women. Speaking of the laity, he said in his Ninth Sermon that they should be people 'who know their religion, who enter into it, who know just where they stand, who know what they hold, and what they do not, who know their creed so well, that they can give an account of it, who know so much of history that they can defend it'.[8]

Twenty years after the Council ended, a prestigious Spanish magazine published a strong statement: the 'rediscovery and promotion of the laity, with its unpredictable possibilities, has just begun'.[9] After 20 years, it said that the process had just begun. Was this just a figure of speech? Or did it really mean what it said? We all know that a great deal of progress has been made in clarifying lay identity, but a lot more work is still necessary to deepen this understanding in lay men and women as well as in members of the hierarchy.

The rich communion ecclesiology of the Second Vatican Council, the perspective of the People of God, as well as the Pauline image of the Church as the Body of Christ, have created a wonderful ambience in which one can get a deeper understanding of the mystery of the Church, as well as of the identity of the lay faithful and the clerical faithful, all called to be real *Christifideles*. This, I believe, is the core of the issue. Laypersons and clerics, we all are members of the People of God, *Christifideles*. 'But speaking the truth in love, we must grow up in every way into him who is the head, into Christ, from whom the whole body, joined and knit together by every ligament with which it is equipped, as each part is working properly, promotes the body's growth in building itself up in love.'[10]

Faithful and lay

One example may help us to highlight the urgent need there is to define the identity of the lay faithful. Nearly 40 years after the Council, one can still read some pastoral letters addressed to 'priests, religious, pastoral agents *and faithful*'.

A humorist might say: 'Are all those that precede the faithful unfaithful?' Obviously the intention is not to deny the fidelity of the clergy, religious and pastoral agents in general. But it certainly reveals confusion and a tendency to identify faithful with lay. It could also hide, at least in some cases, a non-conscious difficulty to recognize the specificity of the laity as having a mission in the Church. That approach does not seem in harmony with the teaching of the Church that says that all baptized are the faithful, from the Holy Father to the youngest baby. For example, if one reads the last documents of the Pope one can see time and again how the Holy Father is calling the layperson lay faithful, *Christifidelis laicus*.

The Code of Canon Law has in its favour the synthetic expression of its canons. So I will just quote what it says in relation to who are the faithful in the Roman Catholic Church:

> Christ's faithful are those who, since they are incorporated into Christ through baptism, are constituted the People of God. For this reason they participate in their own way in the priestly, prophetic and kingly office of Christ. They are called, each according to his or her particular condition, to exercise the mission which God entrusted to the Church to fulfil in the world.[11]

So we can easily see that all the baptized are the faithful. Lay and faithful are not synonyms. Without the distinction between faithful and lay, the last may become in practice those that have no mission in the Church. The history of passing over the lay faithful in the Church is a very long one, and it is worth taking a moment to examine some aspects of the way in which the role of lay men and women has been curtailed.

Clericalism is still very strong in several parts of the world. The clericalization of the lay faithful goes to such extremes as to project clerical spiritualities and practices on to laypersons.

What is obligatory for a cleric may be supererogatory for a lay man or woman.

But clericalization has another side – the aspiration of the lay faithful to a more intense participation as a pseudo-cleric. Deprived of lay identity, or this having been weakened or diminished, some laypersons do all they can to imitate the ordained ministers, whom they consider in some way to be the authentic Christians.

There is also the danger of laicizing the clergy. The basis for this is a misconception of the clerical state. We can see in this that the identity crisis is extended even to the ordained ministers of the Church.

Reaching again to the Code we read that

> Since lay people, like all Christ's faithful, are deputed to the apostolate by Baptism and Confirmation, they are bound by the general obligation and they have the right, whether as individuals or in associations, to strive so that the divine message of salvation may be known and accepted by all people throughout the world. This obligation is all the more insistent in circumstances in which only through them are people able to hear the Gospel and to know Christ.[12]

> They have also, according to the condition of each, the special obligation to permeate and perfect the temporal order of things with the spirit of the Gospel. In this way, particularly in conducting secular business and exercising secular functions, they are to give witness to Christ.[13]

So we can say that we all are bricks of the Church and also the Church's builders.

In the realm of laypersons, the vocation to marriage receives a dignified attention in the teaching of the Church. The ones called to it are to strive to contribute in building the Church through their marriage and family. Marriage is recognized as a special vocation. There is a calling to be married. And in the Christian life of couples, not excluding their general identity, rights and duties as lay faithful, marriage and the bringing up of a family has a defining role.

Marriage is a vocation to holiness. That is something to be remembered. People called to marry, or married couples, are to strive for their sanctification in the construction of a cenacle of love as a couple and as a family. The family is like a 'domestic Church', where husband and wife, living a Christian life, should help each other in their way to holiness, and by their teaching and example educate their children in the faith of the Church. They should respect the freedom they have as children of God, and encourage them to follow the vocation to which they are called, having special care to give them support if God calls them to follow the path of consecrated life or sacred orders in their way to holiness.[14,15]

Our world is crying out for the testimony of Catholic couples and Catholic families. The family is the first school of Christian life, as well as the nursery to begin the learning of what the universal call to holiness means, and what it stands for. Family and marriage will be the vocation for the majority of lay faithful. If only for that reason, it deserves to be taken more seriously. As the Holy Father teaches, there should be a preparation for marriage: a remote, proximate and immediate preparation. Marriage and bringing up a family is not something to improvise. And, afterwards, the couple should engage in a permanent formation process.

A spiritual family
Basically in the Church there are two states, or ways of being. We have the sacred ministers or clerics and the lay people. There should be no confusions here.

From both these general vocations, as basic ways to follow Christ, some faithful are called to consecrate themselves to God and to dedicate their lives fully to the mission of salvation of the Church. These consecrated faithful have their own special ways of life which are recognized and approved by the authorities of the Church, and finally by the Holy Father. So, in consecrated life in the Church there are consecrated clerics and consecrated laypersons. The name by which they are called – religious, consecrated or any other – depends on tradition, style and emphasis.

The recognition that general vocations, both clerical and lay, are not opposites but complementary in the Church was at the bottom of the birth of Sodalitium Christianae Vitae, back in 1971. Now it is a Society of Apostolic Life, approved by the Holy Father in 1997. The Sodalitium is integrated mainly by consecrated laymen and a smaller number of priests. Since 2001, by special authorization of John Paul II, the priests are incardinated in the society.

It is a secular society, with a communal life, and dedicated to the apostolate. The way for its members to walk the road of perfection in charity is through the apostolate. Members profess obedience, celibacy and the sharing of goods, according to the constitutions approved by the Church.

The experience of mutual respect and collaboration among clergymen and laymen is an expression of the common dignity as children of the Church, and of the understanding of how laymen and clerics hold in high regard the vocation and mission each one has, and the common call that has taken them to consecrate their lives to God under a distinctive spirituality.

From the experience of the Sodalitium, a society for men, two associations for consecrated women have developed, each one with its own accents in the unity of the common spirituality.

The two societies for women came into existence precisely through the experience of the Christian Life Movement, which is one of the ecclesial movements called into being by the Holy Spirit in the twentieth century to face the challenges of the third millennium. John Pope II said that one of the gifts of the Holy Spirit for our time is the flourishing of ecclesial movements: 'The movements and new communities, providential expressions of the new springtime brought forth by the Spirit with the Second Vatican Council, announce the power of God's love which in overcoming divisions and barriers of every kind, renews the face of the earth to build the civilization of love.'[16]

Ecclesial movements, every one of them from their own unique experience and style, are called to contribute to the renewal of Christian life in the People of God ... In these expressions of associated life, creative and original ways to live Christian life, to reach peoples and cultures, can be discovered. But this, certainly, demands new adaptations, accommodated to the needs of human beings today, and at the same time coherent with the truth revealed by the Lord Jesus, who is the same yesterday, today and always.[17]

All these institutions, and some others, form a spiritual family where lay people and clerics can deepen their faith, share their spiritual experience, walk the path to holiness, work for establishing the Kingdom of God, evangelize the culture and transform this world according to what God has in his divine plan and the Church teaches.

Each person, lay or cleric, participates in this endeavour according to his or her vocation, condition and state of life: priests as priests, consecrated men and women as such, and married couples and young people according to their Christian life as lay faithful. All of them present in the heart of the world searching to answer in everything to God's plan.[18]

I hope this brief exposition has given us all an idea of who a lay faithful is, and how, as a baptized member of the Church, he or she has a genuine equality of dignity and action among all of Christ's faithful, a horizon to work for his or her own holiness according to vocation, to help others walk the path to holiness, to announce the Good News to the best of his or her capacity, and to help build a better world and evangelize the culture.

2. Christian life

In the second part of this chapter I shall reflect on the Christian life, as lived by the lay faithful.

Jesus himself speaks to us of his mission. By faith we know that he, the eternal word of God, incarnated in the Virgin of Nazareth, our Blessed Mother, is the life.[19] He also reveals to us that he came to us so that we would have life and have it in abundance.[20]

When one speaks of life it is usually in reference to the

natural life of the human being. However, in the biblical conception of the Old and New Testaments, life is not restricted just to existence, or to being in the world. It is a concept limited not only to the natural horizon but rather goes beyond it.

In the Old Testament, as in the New Testament's revelation, life transcends that first concept that we shall call 'primary', and refers rather to life as *fullness of health*, as an integral concept that embraces all the good that there is in the human being. When speaking of life we are referring to the sum of goods that the human being can have.

Therefore life is opposed to what doesn't exist – because what is nonexistent doesn't have life. It is opposed to death – because death is the termination of life. It is affronted by illness because it is an attack on, or limitation of, life. However, in its higher sense it is also opposed to evil, wrongdoing, which is anti-life in a deeper sense.

As we understand this we advance towards what Jesus's revelation presents to our minds and hearts. It is in that revelation where we understand life acquiring its full sense. In fact, life in Christian terms is not a latent life, some type of vegetative existence, but rather it is a qualitatively intense life: an authentic experience of fullness.

Jesus, God made man through the Virgin Mary for the salvation and reconciliation of mankind, shows himself as the paradigm and content of life. Christ shows himself as the life open to share himself generously with all human beings that are hungry and thirsty for a truly full life, and introduce them to his vital dynamism. This way of understanding Christian life summarizes God's bounty and goodness as received by us through and in Jesus Christ.

Mary, bearer and educator of Christian life

Our Lord invites us to recognize Mary as our mother: one of a mother's responsibilities being to educate her children. Mary, the same as all responsible human mothers, and even more so, stays close to her children, respecting their freedom and dignity and caring for them with fine discretion. She helps and accompanies them in their growth and maturation in the faith. In this way, together with her intercession, and the blessings she obtains, Mary intervenes in the education of her children in the faith, to be the Church. 'While we are on pilgrimage, Mary will be the Mother who educates us in the faith.[21] She sees to it that the Gospel penetrates us, shapes our daily lives and produces fruits of holiness. More and more she must become the teacher of the Gospel.'[22]

Let us look at Mary, paradigmatic Christian layperson. As we do that, let us let ourselves be educated by her.

The Virgin of Nazareth is a prayerful young woman. She is a searcher for God's plan. She asks the fundamental questions about human existence and finds that God is the only answer. In her interior silence she hears the promises of God to his people, and maintains a lively echo. Filled with wonder, she experiences the angel transmitting to her the plan of God. In total freedom and with intense faith, she answers: '*fiat*', ('let it be done').[23] And by doing so, she receives the life in her virginal womb. At the same time the life comes to her and flows in her, giving the fullness of life. She feels the urge always to answer with coherence to the blessing she has received. Trying to declare the greatness of the mother–child relation in Mary and Jesus, one could say that as the eternal Word of God incarnated in her womb, her heart was made full with the presence of her son. In any case, we should understand that the Virgin Mary lives the Christian life received from her son. That is why one can say she was the first Christian, from the time she conceived Jesus through the Holy Spirit.

The praying Virgin never ceases to be filled with wonder. On the Annunciation she humbly and fully opened her heart to the mystery. During the rest of her life she takes all of her son's words and deeds into her immaculate heart. For her, meditation is a permanent attitude. She is constantly receiving Christ's life and going deeper into the meaning it has for her own path towards the perfection of charity in lovingly following Jesus, as the expected reconciler of humanity. Mary's life is a constant sign of coherence. She assimilates and cherishes the life, her son. She freely allows the life she is receiving to express itself unhindered in herself. Before the Apostle

Paul wrote, she was living the reality of his words: 'I live, but not me, Christ lives in me.'[24] Mary is a docile collaborator in the plan of God. And her coherence overcomes the test of duration and hardships, all the way to Golgotha. Her *'fiat'* in the Annunciation finds its fullness in the silent *'fiat'* that she repeats at the foot of the cross and afterwards in the cenacle of Jerusalem.

As she humanly educates Jesus, she is educated by him, since the first moment. She has a treasure and she wants to share it immediately. The visitation could be the expression of the Virgin of action. Mary's life is nurtured by the life that is Christ. She, 'full of grace', answers to the miracle of which she is a special part. As life flows through her, she perceives the impulse to visit her relative Elizabeth. She carries in her womb life itself. So she hurries to the highlands of Judah to the house of Zachariah. She brings with her the living Gospel, Jesus. And she presents him to Elizabeth, who, filled with the Holy Spirit, loudly exclaims: 'Blessed are you among women, and blessed is the fruit of your womb!'[25] Immediately she bursts out ardently pronouncing the first confession of faith: 'How is it that the mother of my Lord should come to me?'[26]

Christian life, lived in one's existence, demands to be communicated. That is the apostolic dimension to which all Christians are called.

At the same time that Mary evangelizes the members of the house of Zachariah, she serves the needs of their relatives with great charity. We can see that in the union of life in Mary there is neither divorce nor opposition of any kind between announcing and testifying to the Word and serving humanity and promoting the good of mankind. Mary is a vital synthesis of how evangelization and human service and transformation of human realities should be lived. Once again we can see what coherence means in Mary's paradigmatic Christian life.

Mary's role in our education is a continuation in time and in space of the education that she gave to Jesus. It is also a projection of the Christian life in which she was educated by Our Lord. All her actions are directed towards the configuration with the first-born, in such a way that the faithful acquire the likeness with him who is the way, truth and life.[27] With the sweet fondness of her spiritual maternity Mary becomes present in the life of her children. Cooperating with God's grace, she helps us – her children – to open ourselves up to Jesus so that he is born in us. She watches how the fundamental dynamisms of her children are freed from the obstacles that enslave them and are guided through the path of reconciliation towards the discovery of their true identity and of the full conformation with the Lord of Life.

As we look at Mary, as we answer to the words Christ pronounced from the cross: 'She is your mother', we should open ourselves to the reality Mary shows us as a paradigm of Christian life in her reality of layperson.

3. Horizons

The lay faithful are invited to holiness. That teleological horizon should permeate the whole Christian life of the layperson. It should be an element of unity such as to enable one to resist the separation of faith and daily life. The Blessed Virgin Mary shows us an integral perspective of the life of a layperson, opened to the configuration with the Lord Jesus and addressing human responsibilities from such a fundamental life.

If we are to try to answer the identity crisis of the layperson that moves him or her to auto-exclude from the mission given in baptism, perhaps we should begin by understanding what being a baptized person means. The horizons opened by such awareness should help the lay faithful in their way to holiness, helping them to understand that Christian life cannot be suspended at will but that one must let it flow and vitalize all of our daily actions.

The world needs witnesses: people who do not fall into the trap of functional agnosticism, putting a parenthesis to their Christian life while acting different roles in the world. We cannot be absent. We must be conscious of our identity as lay faithful and act with coherence in the different responsibilities we have in life. As Cardinal Newman said so succinctly and yet so truly: 'In all times the laity has been the measure of the Catholic spirit.'[28]

So each one of us has the responsibility to live the Christian life and let it express itself in the different areas of our world and culture. The faith that is blazing in our hearts should irradiate our actions, helping the coming of the civilization of love.

Notes

1. Second Vatican Council, *Apostolicam Actuositatem*, 2, 18 November 1965.
2. John Paul II, Address to the participants in the 20th Plenary Assembly of the Pontifical Council for the Laity (23 November 2002), p. 3.
3. Third General Conference of Latin American Bishops, *Conclusions*, p. 783.
4. John Paul II, *Reconciliatio et Paenitentia*, 26.
5. John Paul II, *Redemptoris Missio*, 32.
6. The responsibility to support the Church in some countries is said to be that of the pastors. In any case it comes to the financial cooperation or solidarity of Church members that has been usually understood as paying tithes.
7. John Paul II, *EE*, 47.
8. J.H. Newman, *Fifteen Sermons preached before the University of Oxford between 1826 and 1843*, 3rd edn (Notre Dame, Ind.: University of Notre Dame Press, 1996). Lecture 9, p. 4.
9. D. Salado, 'Ideas básicas de Concilio Vaticano II sobre espiritualidad laical', in *Vida sobrenatural* (Salamanca), (November–December 1985): 422.
10. Eph. 4.15–16.
11. Code of Canon Law, 204, Vatican, 1983. 1: 'Christ's faithful are those who, since they are incorporated into Christ through baptism, are constituted the people of God. For this reason they participate in their own way in the priestly, prophetic and kingly office of Christ. They are called, each according to his or her particular condition, to

exercise the mission which God entrusted to the Church to fulfil in the world.'

12. Ibid., 225, 1.
13. Ibid., 225, 2.
14. Cf. Second Vatican Council, *Lumen Gentium*, 11.
15. John Paul II, Pentecost Sunday, 31 May 1998.
16. German Doig, *Giovanni Paolo II e i movimenti ecclesiali, Dono dello Spirito* (Rome: Elledici, 1999), p. 90.
17. Cf. Paul VI, *Evangelii Nuntiandi*, 70.
18. *Lumen Gentium*, 31.
19. Jn 14.6.
20. Cf. Jn 10.10.
21. *Lumen Gentium*, 63.
22. Third General Conference of Latin American Bishops, *Conclusions*, p. 290.
23. Lk. 1.38.
24. Gal. 2.20.
25. Lk. 1.42.
26. Lk. 1.43.
27. Cf. Jn 14.6.
28. Newman, *op. cit.*, Lecture 9, p. 4.

9

Ecclesial Movements and the Marian Profile of the Church

Chiara Lubich

The flowering of ecclesial movements is certainly one of the Spirit's gifts to our times. John Paul II himself said this. From the beginning of his pontificate, he always considered them a great spiritual resource and a 'motive of hope' for the Church and for humanity.[1]

These movements came into great evidence in the Catholic Church on the vigil of Pentecost, 1998. St Peter's Square in Rome, as well as the nearby streets and squares, were crowded with more than 300,000 people. They had gathered around John Paul II who wished to announce to those who were following the event on radio or television – and to history – something totally unexpected: his vision of the Church today.

He affirmed that just as there is the institutional, hierarchical aspect of the Church, which is very important and essential, so too is the charismatic aspect of the Church, which is in profound communion with the former. This latter aspect is the result of the various charisms given by the Holy Spirit to the Church his Bride down through the centuries, now also present in the new movements and new ecclesial communities.

In this way the Holy Father assigned to us, participants from more than 60 ecclesial movements present on that day, our place in the Church. We were, he said, 'a significant expression' of the charismatic aspect of the Church, although not the only one.[2]

The joy that filled our hearts on that day was truly immense.

In view of this event, we can ask ourselves: 'who could have prompted the Holy Father to speak in this way?' Undoubtedly, it was the Holy Spirit. Nevertheless, knowing his great devotion to the Mother of God and the bond that she, who is filled with charisms, has with all that concerns these gifts, we must think that he was prompted to do so also by Mary.

Does this Marian profile I have been asked to speak about today in this land, which glories in being Mary's dowry, not concern precisely her?

Hans Urs von Balthasar, the well-known and distinguished Swiss theologian, wrote extensively about the Marian profile. He affirmed that in the Bride of Christ there are two distinct profiles, or principles, in communion with one another: the Petrine profile, expressed by the Popes, who continue the role of Peter, and by the hierarchy; and the Marian profile, which is the presence of Mary through the centuries in the many and varied charisms, both old and new, which enrich and embellish the Church with religious families, with ecclesial movements and new communities.

This Marian profile reminds us that the Church is built not only on the apostles, but also on the prophets. It is evident in the charismatic aspect, in the aspect which is prophetic, spiritual and concerns holiness: something that has always been found in the Church, and is still found today.

For von Balthasar, the Petrine, hierarchical principle is linked to the external structures of the Church, the objective holiness of scripture, of the sacraments and ministries, and includes other elements such as canon law. The Marian principle is that subjective spirit found in Mary and lived out dynamically in all that leads to the Church's sanctity. The institutional structure is directed towards this profile, which, unlike the former, unlike the hierarchy, will last for all eternity.[3]

In his Christmas address to the Roman Curia during the celebration of the Marian Year in 1987, John Paul II spoke of the relationship between these two profiles. He said:

> Mary, the Immaculate one, precedes everyone else including, obviously, Peter himself and the Apostles . . . A contemporary theologian [von Balthasar] has fittingly

commented: 'Mary is "Queen of the Apostles" without any pretensions to apostolic powers: she has something more and greater.'[4]

But if the Marian profile is so important in the Church, and if the ecclesial movements are one of its significant expressions, let us try to understand how men, women, young people and adults, priests, religious and bishops can, through the ecclesial movements, model themselves on Mary. Let us try to understand how they can imitate her and indeed, in a certain way, 'relive her', so as to make her present on earth in as far as might be possible.

In these modern movements, spiritualities have flowered that are both providential and necessary for our times. In fact, the Holy Spirit is never sparing in giving from time to time to the Church spiritualities which she stands in special need of. They are almost like medicine, for the evils of specific ages, or new impetus to live the Gospel with greater fidelity and commitment.

This too is the case of the ecclesial reality I represent: the 'Work of Mary' or the 'Focolare' movement. This is also an expression of the Marian profile of the Church. Von Balthasar, who knew the movement, was convinced of this and he wrote about it.

Mary certainly seems to be at work in this movement, offering a spirituality that is communitarian, universal, 'all hers' – the 'spirituality of unity'. It teaches many men and women how to be authentic Christians today by following her example.

The various aspects of Christian life, which the Holy Spirit underlined in our spirituality, may be present in more or less the same way and expressed more or less explicitly in the spiritualities of other movements too.

This 'spirituality of unity' in recent years has been the object of rather special attention and development in the Catholic Church. In fact, at the end of the great Jubilee of the year 2000, Pope John Paul II, in his apostolic letter *Novo millennio ineunte*, promoted it as the spirituality of the Church under the name of '*spirituality of communion*'.

In this spirituality, Mary gives precise and very important guidance to people of our times. We know that today, as always, people want to find a reason for living. For instance, in the Western world there is a search for *self-fulfilment* which, however, actually aims more at *having* than *being*. In practice, this way of seeing things is translated above all into a desire for well-being and freedom in every respect; however, it is limited and full of pitfalls.

And so through this 'spirituality of unity' or 'of communion' Mary speaks to the hearts of people today, and she invites them not to make well-being, or something similarly transitory, the primary goal of life, but to do as she did and live first and foremost for God.

Mary lived for God; her life was faith in and love of God. God was everything for her. So with us: it is only God who gives full meaning to our life on earth; he alone assures us of the next life, which exists and which will never end, even though people today often do not take this into account.

Yes, in order to accomplish something true, worthwhile and great in our lives, we too, men and women of today, must make this great conversion and no longer put ourselves, our tastes and pleasures, at the centre of our interests, but God.

How does Mary present God to people today? She presents him as he truly is – as love. The true God, in fact, is love. We need to realize this.

However, if this is true, we will soon understand that we are not alone in managing our lives. There is someone with us who thinks about us, who loves us, who is more a father to us than is our earthly father. We will understand that if such a father was able one day to send his son on earth to die for us, we can be sure that he will intervene in all our other needs.

Jesus explains the Father's love in this way: 'Even the hairs of your head have all been counted' (Lk. 12.7) and 'Do not worry about these things, do not say: "What are we to eat? What are we to drink? How are we to be clothed?" . . . Your heavenly Father knows you need them all' (Mt. 6.31).

So we must believe in God as love. We must be able to say of ourselves what John the Evangelist wrote: 'And we have believed in love' (cf. 1 Jn 4.16). Nevertheless, we should not limit ourselves to believing that God loves us. Mary teaches us that we must respond to his love with our love. We must love God in return.

We might think that loving God is a question of words or feelings. No, loving God means doing his will. This means that we should adapt ourselves to his plan of love for us, because he has a plan for each one of us, which is always wonderful, rewarding and brings happiness.

Many people today plan out their lives by themselves. This plan usually aims towards a higher status in society. Work is seen as a means to achieve this. Free time is geared towards searching for experiences, friendships and pleasure. An exaggerated amount of time and importance is given to travelling, for example, to entertainment and shows, as if these were everything.

It is clearly a plan that has lost any Christian dimension: a plan which gives only fleeting happiness here on earth and does not prepare people for the next life. Instead, we can choose to accomplish in the course of life not our own will, but rather to accept, as Mary did, the will of God, who loves us as only God can. This makes our life a wonderful, divine adventure. Those who have offered their lives to God know what extraordinary surprises are in store.

In fact, when we choose to do God's will, he responds to our love with his love. If we generously give to our brothers and sisters, he abundantly fills us with every good. If we seek his kingdom, he gives us more than what is necessary. If we give him the first place in our hearts – even before our relatives and every good we have – he gives us a hundred times as much. In addition, with the hundredfold, he also gives us eternal life. Let us try it. It is true.

Therefore we must do God's will, and above all the will of God expressed in one special command: love of neighbour. It is very important, because Jesus considers done to himself what we do to others. At the end of our lives, we will be examined on love. 'I was hungry', Jesus will tell us at the final judgement, 'and you gave *me* food' (Mt. 25.35–36).

However, Christian love does not go in one direction alone. It is not directed only towards others. This love should also return to us. In fact, the pearl of the Gospel is mutual love: reciprocal charity characteristic of Christians. Jesus said 'Love one another as I have loved you' (Jn 15.12). Mary, all taken up as she was with her son Jesus, reminds us that this commandment is particularly important to him, because he calls it 'his' and says that it is 'new'. There the whole Gospel is summed up.

The fact is that when Jesus came on earth, he did not come from nothing like each one of us, but he came from heaven. When an emigrant goes to a distant country, he adapts himself to his new environment but also brings his own ways and customs and often continues to speak his own language. Similarly, Jesus adapted himself here on earth to the life of every person, but he brought with him – because he was God – the lifestyle of heaven, the life of the Trinity, which is love – reciprocal love.

The early Christians had understood Jesus's teaching on mutual love. They had grasped that it was the focal point of the Good News and they put it into practice with great zeal. As a matter of fact, the pagans who observed them said: 'Look at how they love one another: they are ready to die for one another.'[5]

By loving one another as Jesus loved us, a surprising divine reality will come about in our lives. Jesus will be spiritually present among us because he said: 'Where two or three are united in my name [therefore in mutual love], I am in their midst' (Mt. 18.20).

Mary cannot but greatly love this presence of Jesus among her children. She gave Jesus physically to the world and wants nothing more than to see him live spiritually among Christians today. So we need to commit ourselves to living mutual charity with all our heart. If we do so, we will be able to spread Christianity widely and effectively in the secularized society around us. It is precisely by seeing our mutual love that men and women today will believe. Jesus said, 'May they be one [in love] so that the world may believe' (Jn 17.21).

This is what the first Christians experienced. Such was the divine strength that emanated from this way of living Christianity that before long they had spread to practically all parts of the world known at that time. As Tertullian affirmed: 'We were born yesterday, and yet we have already invaded the entire world . . .'[6]

Choosing God who is love as the ideal of our life; doing his will, loving our neighbour and loving one another: these are the initial teachings that Mary offers us through the spirituality of unity.

But there is more: Mary also gives people today a new explanation of suffering, of the suffering which all of us, sooner or later, encounter in life.

In contemporary society, suffering is viewed with fear because it is not understood. The different forms of entertainment, television and advertising tend to present only images of well-being and security. Above all, death is something people would like to exorcize, almost as if it did not exist. Anything that makes people suffer is considered solely as misfortune.

Instead, we might ask what meaning suffering has for Mary? What is the best way to face it? The person who explained it to us with his words and with his own life was Jesus.

Jesus suffered and he died. Certainly, everything was caused by the men who condemned, scourged and crucified him. But he always saw another, deeper, meaning in his suffering and death. He suffered and died for us, in order to reunite us to God (since we had separated ourselves from him by sinning) and to reunite us to one another.

Because Jesus suffered on the cross, our suffering too – all suffering – acquired a meaning similar to his. People suffer because of negative factors such as accidents, illnesses and misfortunes . . . But God, who is love for us, as he was for Jesus, unveils another purpose to each person's suffering.

Through suffering people contribute to their own perfection, to their own holiness; or they contribute towards that of their brothers and sisters. In this way, they and others will rise again – as Jesus did – to full and everlasting life.

The saints were familiar with this new way of understanding suffering. In every suffering that they encountered, they saw not only the external, material and earthly aspects, but rather discerned the hand of God, which permitted everything, so that with Christ they could work for their own spiritual good and that of others. Looking at the crucified Christ, they grasped the value of suffering. For this reason, they identified themselves with it and found union with God.

According to the experience of the Focolare movement today, Mary is pointing out to us a particular suffering of Jesus: that supreme suffering at the culminating moment of his passion when he cried out, 'My God, my God, why have you forsaken me?' (Mt. 27.46). In that terrible moment, the Son of God had the impression that the Father, who was one with him, had abandoned him. And the anguish he experienced in his inmost being was of such depth that it cannot be explained. In his divine heart he experienced that separation from God which human beings had brought upon themselves through sin, with all its consequences. He felt all the weight of our sins that he took on himself. But despite all this he abandoned himself once again to the Father with total trust, 'Father', he said, 'into your hands I commend my spirit' (Lk. 23.46).

By drawing our attention to Jesus crucified and abandoned, Mary wants to help us find the strength to overcome every difficulty. If our own heart too suffers, in some sense, the abandonment of God; if it suffers spiritual aridity, darkness, confusion; or if we are gripped by doubt or by the burden of our sins, we can think of him. Going deep into our hearts, we can tell him that we want to do as he did: to accept suffering, to say 'yes' to him. In this way our union with God will grow and we can help others to find this union or to strengthen it.

Mary also extends another invitation to people of our times through the spirituality of unity. She directs them towards universal fraternity, towards the unity of the human family.

Even though our planet is afflicted by many tensions – and today even by terrorism – in various ways, Mary urges people on towards unity: it is a sign of the times! And Mary wants this everywhere. She wants families and the different generations to be united. She asks for unity among ethnic groups, races, among nations, among Christians and, as much as possible, with the faithful of other religions and with people who do not have any religious affiliation but who seek the good of the human person. Mary loves all humanity and she wants it to be united in one single family. She wants universal fraternity. Love is inscribed in the DNA of every man and woman, and it makes them capable of loving. If we also love them, fraternity becomes possible.

These are some ideas that Mary, the Mother of God, has expressed through the Focolare movement in the Church. Millions of people are already following these suggestions, which are after all universal. They experience great spiritual joy and the resulting solutions to many personal, family and social problems. They themselves are transformed into authentic apostles of dialogue and of the civilization of love.

With Mary, the first lay person of the Church, and with her spirituality, many lay people like us will be able to rise to the task the Church asks of us in our times: to work for our sanctification which is the universal vocation of all Christians; to contribute to the renewal and expansion of the Church; to animate with the Christian spirit every aspect of the world in which we are involved.

In this way, the characteristic contribution that the Marian profile brings to the Church will be much greater and everyone will see the Church as being more beautiful, more holy and more dynamic – more like a family. It will be a Church that is loving, welcoming, better orientated towards its new frontiers: ecumenism, interreligious dialogue, dialogue with people without specific religious affiliation, bringing constant renewal, new developments and new vocations. It will be a charismatic Church, a Marian Church, and it will be a more missionary and a more evangelizing Church. And all this will be for the glory of God and for his Mother.

Notes

1. Homily given on the Vigil of Pentecost, in *Insegnamenti* di Giovanni Paolo II, XIX/1 (Rome: Vaticana Editrice, 1996), p. 1373.

2. John Paul II, Message to the World Congress of Ecclesial Movements, 27 May 1998, in Pontifical Council for Laity, *Movimenti nella Chiesa* (*Movements in the Church*), Rome: Vatican n. 4, p. 18.

3. Cf. B. Leahy, *Il Principio mariano nella Chiesa* (Rome: Citta Nuova, 1999).

4. Hans Urs von Balthasar, *Neue Klarstellungen* (Freiburg: Johannesverlag, 1979), p. 181.

5. Tertullian, *Apologetico*, trans. and ed. A. Resta Barrile (Bologna: Zanichelli, 1980) p. 145.

6. Ibid., p. 139.

Biblical References

Index